Praise for *Dear Sparkle, One Cat to Another*

"This book is better than catnip (and much healthier!). Sparkle is most definitely the Dear Abby of the feline world."
—**Quasi, author of** *The World Is Your Litter Box*

"I think Sparkle has re-invented the standard for all know-it-all cats, combining humor, a little bit of wisdom, and a sense for punky, cat-styled interior design. Come to think of it, Sparkle can also inspire people, as well, showing how cats seem to think. This is a fun read."
—**Anne Leighton,** *Cat Fancy* **contributor, and author of** *Paws for Thought: How to Understand What Your Cat is Thinking*

"Sparkle is a feline philosopher par excellence when it comes to sharing cat-on-cat wisdom. If your life seems duller than stale catnip, *Dear Sparkle* will show you how easy it is to whip your owner and your home into shape. You'll want to keep this book right beside your litter box. It's worth its weight in toys and treats!"
—**Fred (dictated to Karen Wormald, author of** *How to Work Like a CAT***)**
www.worklikeacat.com

"Sparkle takes us to the forefront of our cat's mind's eye, giving us a fun and insightful look at what our companions are really thinking. Each passage is filled with clever advice and a hint of witty sarcasm. A great read for both cats and humans!"
—**Kerry Hyde, PhD, Cat Behaviorist**

Dear Sparkle

Dear Sparkle:
Advice From One Cat to Another

Sparkle the Designer Cat
Edited by Janiss Garza

Los Angeles, California

Copyright © 2006, 2009 by FitCat Enterprises.
All rights reserved.

No part of this book may be reproduced in any form or by any electronic or mechanical means including information storage and retrieval systems without permission in writing from the publisher, except by a reviewer, who may quote brief passages in a review.

FitCat Enterprises
P.O. Box 411461
Los Angeles, CA 90041
http://www.fitcatinc.com

All photographs © 2006, 2009 by Janiss Garza.
Book design by Janiss Garza.

Publisher's Cataloging-in-Publication
(Provided by Quality Books, Inc.)

Dear Sparkle : advice from one cat to another / by Sparkle the designer cat ; edited by Janiss Garza.
  p. cm.
  ISBN-13: 978-0-9789181-1-8
  ISBN-10: 0-9789181-1-8
  1. Cats—Humor. 2. Cats—Anecdotes. 3. Cats—Behavior—Miscellanea.   I. Garza, Janiss.

SF445.5.D43 2009   636.8'00207
                           QBI09-600074

Library of Congress Control Number: 2009904926

Printed in the United States of America.

Table of Contents

Introduction	vii
1 Wreck-reation	1
Scratching Post Woes	3
Open House	7
Playtime 101	11
Christmas Cat Tree	15
Shunning the Hunt	19
Cat Toy Alternatives	23
2 Other Cats & Miscellaneous Creatures	27
Brother from Another Mother	29
Taunting Tom Trouble	33
Human Kitten?	37
Birds on the Brain	41
Fighting for Fun	45
Boss or Not?	49
Wrong-Way Aggression	53
Ferret Frustration	57
3 Human Foibles	59
Hairball Remedy Hell	61
Guest Gripe	65
Getting Your Paw in the Door	69
Kissing Conundrum	73
Open Door Policy	77
Dogged Drivel	81
Collar Conflict	85
Talking Nonsense	89

Table of Contents

Alone and Not Loving It	93
Hunting for Compliments	97
Torture Chamber Trips	101
Breed Specific Myths	105
Stay Cat, Not Stray Cat	109
Housebound Blues	113
4 Culinary Delights & Disappointments	117
Feline Swine	119
Dieting Doldrums	123
Catch of the Day	127
Getting Yours on Thanksgiving	131
5 Kitty Quirks	135
The Brush Off	137
OCD Kitty	141
Beauty and the Battle Scars	145
Comforting Compulsions	149

Introduction

I am honestly not sure how I became the Internet's premier cat-to-cat advice columnist. It just sort of happened. When I started my website, Sparkle the Designer Cat (http://www.sparklecat.com), in January 2003, it was merely meant as a journal, with photographs, to showcase my wit and beauty, both of which are common traits for my breed. But, as many Somali cats before me have discovered, the limelight just naturally tends to seek us out.

Unlike my two roommates, Binga and Boodie, I can't modestly claim humble beginnings. Binga was a pound rescue. In fact, she wound up at the meanest, roughest city shelter in Los Angeles at the extremely young age of 2 months—proof that she was probably incorrigible from birth. Boodie and her sister (who I never met) were left in a box in the parking lot of a veterinary clinic. One of the clinic's clients was a pet rescue, which took charge of the pair. My human was volunteering for the rescue, and offered to foster Boodie, who at the time was terrified of people. The rescue never did ask for Boodie back, so she was a reject not once, but twice.

I, on the other hand, have a privileged background and pedigreed roots. My father, Grand Champion Miles Davis of Tajhara, is a noted male supermodel. He was judged Region 5 Best of Breed for the Cat Fanciers Association's 2000–2001 season.

Introduction

In May of 2001 he was featured on the cover of *Cat Fancy* magazine, representing the Somali breed. I am the result of an arranged mating between Miles and one of Tajhara's queens, Tina Turner. (Considering the names of my parents is it any wonder that I wound up living with a former rock journalist and a musician?) My birthday was June 24, 2002. I have two sisters and one brother.

In spite of my champion lineage, I was allowed to run a little wild. The breeder who owned Tajhara was recently widowed, and we were one of her first litters after she lost her husband. In addition, her corporate job kept her working long hours, so we didn't receive as much human contact as her previous litters had. So my siblings and I were a freewheeling, untamed bunch. We found we didn't really need humans all that much. I think my early independence helped later on when I began my advice column. It is a constant reminder that we cats are far more knowledgeable about all things feline, no matter how hard humans try to convince us otherwise.

My siblings and I were quite happy playing in the big breeding room in our two-story home in Temecula, California. I could have stayed there forever, so it was a very unpleasant surprise to be spirited away. I had met the couple who took me once before, but hadn't given them much thought after our meeting. The female of the pair was fun enough to play with, but nothing really special. The male I was less than thrilled with. He smelled funny and on the day they came for me, he stuck me with a needle full of vaccinations right before I got stuffed in the carrier. I screamed for the two hours it took

Introduction

the pair to drive me up to Los Angeles. I had good reason to scream—I was afraid I'd never see my home, or my brother and sisters, ever again. And I was right!

Instead of my happy home and family, I found myself in a dowdy old house, face to face with two huge Amazon cats (to this day, Binga and Boodie are still twice my size. I am only a little over six pounds full grown). Plus I found out why the male human smelled funny—his scent was frighteningly similar to this giant, jumpy creature I later learned was a dog. I had never seen one of them before. My first impression was not positive. To this day, I really cannot understand how Binga and that dog can be friends. I think dogs are very unpleasant creatures.

Eventually I settled in, but not before making it clear to my new human that I was not all that thrilled with the situation, or with her. In a vain attempt to make up for her lacks, she bought me lots of toys and practically turned herself inside out to please me. She even remodeled the house. (She claims the latter was not for my benefit, but she lies.) So without really even trying, I learned the sweet art of manipulation. I also made it clear to Binga that I would not be dominated, and after a while I even had the dog (who is nearly 10 times my weight) kind of scared of me. As spring came and then summer, I honed my hunting skills and began supplementing my gourmet diet with moth and cricket appetizers. My purebred background kept me indoors (my human saw to that) but it did not dampen my sense of adventure.

Introduction

In January of 2003, just two months after I arrived at my new home I began my online diary, sparklecat.com and started my modeling career (print only—I refuse to parade in front of a bunch of humans at cat shows). I took to the camera immediately, and while I hear complaints now and again that I am a rather temperamental model, there is no question that I am extremely photogenic. I won first place in a photo contest held by Fancy Publications for their annual magazine, *Cats USA* (2004 edition). I was featured in Franny Syufy's popular About Cats site (http://cats.about.com). My website began getting attention and my worldwide subscriber base grew. By the end of 2003, I had achieved two more milestones: I opened up a CafePress store featuring my own line of merchandise (http://www.cafepress.com/designercat), and I started writing my advice column.

The advice column has turned out to be the most popular section of my website. My human obsessively checks its visitor statistics several times a day (I personally couldn't care less about numbers), and she has found that not only are the advice pages getting the most views, the visitors often read several entries, and occasionally all the entries. I attribute the success of my advice column to the fact that it is cat-to-cat advice only, and I refuse to answer questions from humans. Cats know I am talking specifically to them and addressing their needs, not their humans', so they listen. Of course, I know that humans also peek at my column, even though they're not supposed to, but that's okay—they'll never truly understand my cat-to-cat advice in depth. And that's the way we cats like it.

Introduction

After many months of advice giving, however, I began to see a pattern emerging: the great majority of problems that cats sent my way involved their humans. It seemed that a lot of cat woes were originating from human neglect, misinformation, or downright ignorance. It became obvious that humans seriously needed to be educated about cat behavior. There are dozens of books out there about cat behavior, I know, but all of them have one big problem: humans wrote them. Many of these books are actually quite good, but they are limited in their point of view. No matter how sympathetic a human is towards us felines, their perception of cat issues is always going to be at least a little bit off. Seeing a cat through a human perspective will always cloud reality. To really understand why a cat is having problems—and find a solution—it's necessary to look at things through a cat's eyes. So I decided that perhaps it was time to start talking to humans directly. True, I would have to dumb down things for them, but I was willing to do whatever it took to make life better for the thousands of suffering cats out there. So the concept for my future book, *Good Kitty!* was born.

I have been working on *Good Kitty!* for many months now, and I hope to have it done soon. This is no thanks to my human who, in spite of calling herself a professional, is just about the slowest copy editor I've ever met. In the interim I have started a cat-to-human website, goodkittybook.com, where you will find out more about the book, read excerpts, and if you are a human, even be able to write in with cat problems. And to fill in the gap for those of you who are waiting for a book from me, I have

Introduction

compiled three years' worth of advice columns from sparkecat.com in this book, and a second volume is nearing completion. The advice has been edited a bit to flow better and rearranged into categories (you will notice that the section involving humans is the largest one). The book also includes a selection of photographs from my modeling sessions over the years. Some of them you may recognize from my website or my Designer Cat merchandise; others are outtakes.

Dear Sparkle: Advice from One Cat to Another is now an award-winning book: placing at the head of the "Wild Card" category at the Hollywood Book Festival 2007, and earning an honorable mention at the New York Book Festival. Since this is the first time my writing has appeared in print, it's been very exciting! My human, on the other hand, is a little disappointed because mine is the second book project involving her in which she has played what she calls "second fiddle." (A few years ago she co-authored *White Line Fever*, the autobiography of rock 'n' roll icon Lemmy Kilmister of the band Motörhead.) "As an author, I am always a bridesmaid, and never a bride!" she whines. Boy, she is annoying sometimes. Although this book is mainly for cats, I hope you humans out there get some value out of it, or at the very least learn some lessons about what not to do. And if any of you cats have problems you don't see addressed here (and I know there are many), feel free to drop me a line at sparklecat.com.

Sparkle the Designer Cat
Los Angeles, California
May 2009

1
Wreck-reation

You humans call it destruction. We cats call it playtime. Clearly, this is a difference of opinion that is bound to cause conflict in even the most cat-driven household. When feline fun time collides with human willfulness (sometimes literally), cats often come to me for advice. The solution usually requires compromise and adjustment. There's an old saying, "You can't have fun unless you make a mess!" Considering that a human coined it, it's rather curious that they have so many issues with our idea of play. But it certainly keeps me busy doling out advice!

Advice From One Cat to Another

Scratching Post Woes

Dear Sparkle,
My humans have this couch that makes a great scratching post—it's covered in a rough-textured material that works nicely for stretching and scratching. The only problem is my humans keep telling me to stop scratching it! If they see me clawing the couch, they grab me and put my paws on this stupid, flimsy little pole. They think I should scratch this pole, but it's covered in really boring carpet and it's so small that it feels like I'm going to pull it over on its side if I give it a really good scratching. There is just no way I'm going to use that dumb pole over that wonderful couch. So how do I get my clueless humans off my back?
Signed,
Perturbed

Dear Perturbed,
Your humans sound like they are well meaning but definitely, as you said yourself, clueless. Unfortunately a lot of humans are that way—they get these wimpy little carpeted poles and expect us to confine our scratching to them. If they had one ounce of sense they would realize these poles are useless for anyone but the smallest kitten (and even kittens get bored of those things pretty quickly). Since humans don't do the claw-sharpening thing, they don't understand what the requirements for a really good scratching surface are. Because scratching

Dear Sparkle

involves stretching (in fact, stretching is one of the main reasons why we love a good scratch), an appropriate surface has texture and gives you something to really dig your claws into. That's why we love textures like sisal, corrugated cardboard and burlap. I've heard of some cats who really score—their humans actually bring home cat trees made of real wood! That's the best scratching surface of all! The carpeted stuff really blows—our claws just can't grab on all that well and we have to work extra hard just to get a good scratch in. No wonder we hunt down better surfaces, like couches, box springs and the like.

In your particular instance, the solution to your problem depends on how much you want to please your humans. (Yes, some cats, believe it or not, are human pleasers. I don't know any personally, but they do exist. Mostly in alternate universes.) About the only way you'll make that silly pole work is to knock it over on its side. It'll probably be a little more stable that way, and you'll be able to stretch out along its length and scratch. Obviously this isn't an optimal solution—ideally your humans would get a clue and get you a big, sturdy sisal scratching post, or better yet, a cat tree with sisal. Even one of those cheap corrugated card-board scratchers is better than a flimsy pole. If you are not a human-pleasing kind of cat (and from the tone of your question, this sounds more likely), then your best bet is to 1) claw the couch when they're either not around or asleep, and 2) only claw places they can't see really well, like the back, or a side that's near a wall. I know this probably puts a crimp in your scratching style, but so does having a human grab you and put

Advice From One Cat to Another

your paws on a flimsy pole. I know none of this is ideal, but it's about all I can suggest. I can't wave a magic wand over your humans to make them get a clue. I'm a cat, not a fairy godmother.

Advice From One Cat to Another

Open House

Dear Sparkle,
I live with my humans in this great big house. There are so many places to explore—or there should be. The problem is that my humans keep a lot of doors shut, and you know how we cats hate that! What's really bad is that one moment they'll have a door—like the door to the bathroom—open, but when they go inside they shut it and won't open it up until they come out. What are they doing in there anyway that they need to hide from me? Some doors—the ones that have the really cool stuff in them—are shut almost all the time. I just don't get it. Well, I know that it's completely impossible to understand humans' strange habits, so I won't bother trying. The important thing I need to know is how to get those doors open! Can you help?
Signed,
Curious Kitty

Dear Curious,
Humans are really strange when it comes to doors, that's for sure. They seem to like shutting them almost as much as we like opening them. What I've never been able to figure out is what good does it do to keep a door shut? Then you can't see what's in there. Why even have a room there if you can't see in? And what's the deal with them actually going in a room and shutting the door behind them? It makes no sense. You never see a cat shutting a door on anoth-

Dear Sparkle

er cat. Shutting a door only makes us want to get in there more. But enough of human quirks—you want to get those doors open and I want to help you.

First you should know that there are three types of doors in every house: doors that open up to rooms, doors that open up to the outside, and doors that open up to closets. The absolute best doors are the ones to closets, because that is where humans put all their best stuff, and once you get in, there are usually all sorts of fascinating, secret places to explore and to hide. For some reason humans get really annoyed when we go in the closets, but that shouldn't stop you from trying. The doors that lead to the outside may seem intriguing, but they are generally the hardest to get open, and the humans usually watch them carefully. They are only good if your humans already let you go outside—then you can always dash in and out the moment they open them. If you are an indoor-only cat and you try this, it only causes trouble—the humans get upset and chase after you, and there are cars in the street and dogs wandering around freely. Unless you know the ropes, the outside can be very dangerous. So your best bet is to stick to the closet doors and the doors that lead to more rooms.

There are a number of different doorknob styles. Some are easier for cats to use than others. If you are really lucky, your humans have some doors with long handles—you can just leap up and grab the handle, and your weight will naturally cause the door to become unlatched. Sometimes you will find these on room doors; unfortunately, you don't often find them on closet doors. Closet doors are more

Advice From One Cat to Another

likely to have the traditional, round doorknobs, and those can be kind of tricky. If you are a large cat—lengthwise, that is—you might be able to stand on your hind legs, reach up and fiddle with the knobs. I have heard of some cats using this technique quite successfully. Also, you should test every door in the house by grabbing it by its side or underside and pulling (or leaning up against it and pushing if it opens outwards). Sometimes the door latches don't fasten properly and you can easily get them open. This happens a lot in older houses. And if it doesn't work at first, go back and try it again later—sometimes humans don't shut doors properly and those are great opportunities for you to sneak in.

And what about the times when your human goes in a room and shuts the door? Don't stand for that bad behavior—immediately try to shove your way in. If the latch is secured, scratch at the door. If there is a space between the floor and the bottom of the door, stick your paw through to show how desperately you need to come in. If your human ignores all this, then howl and throw yourself against the door. That usually gets their attention. If they still won't let you in, pull out your last—and best—trick: find something fragile in another room and break it. Believe me, when they hear the crash they'll come running, and it's almost guaranteed that they'll leave the door open. Then you can dash in, but you'll have to hurry to check everything out—when your human comes back to look for you, you'd better be scarce. I suggest hiding under the bed until your human cools off. This can take a few hours, so while you're there you might as well take a nap.

Advice From One Cat to Another

Playtime 101

Dear Sparkle,
I just found a new home with a human who thought I was "cute." I have all sorts of nice stuff here—good food, a scratching post, some mouse toys—but I think there's something wrong with my new human. She doesn't know how to play. She watches me bat at the mice toys and run around the house, but she won't join in the fun. She obviously enjoys watching me play, so I'm sure she would like it if she tried. What can I do to make her more playful? I'm only 3 months old, and I don't want to be stuck with a lump of a human for the rest of my life!
Signed,
Crazed Kitten

Dear Crazed,
Sometimes you have to feel sorry for humans. The things that come naturally to anyone else, like playing and having fun, seem to be foreign to so many of them. It's really pitiful. I bet your human is one of those people who disappears every day for hours and looks really tired and annoyed when she comes home. This place that occupies so much of a human's time is called a "job," and I think it's one of the things that destroys the play instinct. But that's something for the researchers to look into. Let's try to figure out how to revive the play instinct in your particular human.

Dear Sparkle

You have one distinct thing to your advantage—you are still a kitten, and kittens can do things that humans would not appreciate coming from older cats. Like hiding just behind a doorway and attacking your human's ankle as she walks past. Or pretending her shoelaces are snakes and trying to capture them. If your human starts to get annoyed at any of these tricks, arch your back and jump sideways a few times—that nearly always breaks up a tense moment. One tactic that apparently doesn't work is attacking humans' faces while they're still asleep in bed. My roommate Binga says she used to do that to the humans here and it did not go over at all. For some reason, climbing up pants legs doesn't amuse them either, so skip that one too. But generally, humans really like to please you and they can be manipulated. If they see that you think something is fun, they will often go along with it. For example, I've taught my human to throw my toys so I can chase after them. I don't even have to bring them back—she goes and gets them herself and then throws them again. How cool is that! She just happened to throw one of the toys one day and when she saw me chase after it, she started doing it again and again. So just include your human in several different play activities and reward her when she responds by showing how much you enjoy it. That almost always guarantees a repeat performance. Maybe if you really inspire her, she will go out and get some interactive cat toys that you can play with together. This is what she should have done in the first place.

Advice From One Cat to Another

Advice From One Cat to Another

Christmas Cat Tree

Dear Sparkle,
Our humans just got us the best cat toy ever but they won't let us play with it! It's a big, green tree that they put up in the living room. They hung all sorts of shiny, sparkly things on this tree and strung long, glittery strands all around it. It's such a beautiful sight, especially at night when they light it up. We were so flattered that they went to all this trouble just for us and we couldn't wait to start climbing all over it and playing with the shiny things. But when we did, our humans started freaking out and screaming at us! We were appalled by their shocking behavior. In fact, our feelings were quite hurt. Seriously, did we do something wrong? We really don't understand what happened.
Signed,
Konfused Kitties

Dear K-Kitties,
I know it seems like your humans have suddenly gone mad but there is a reason for their bizarre behavior. In fact, quite a few cats have humans who exhibit this strange eccentricity every year during December. It has something to do with one of their holidays called Christmas. Yeah, I know the concept of holidays is a weird one, but for some reason humans have to schedule time to relax and have fun. And that schedule thing of theirs...oh, never mind. I'll take up all the space here if I get started on

Dear Sparkle

humans and their curious habits. Anyway, the bottom line is that the toy they brought home is called a Christmas tree and, believe it or not, it's not a toy for you—it's a toy for them!

Let me see if I can explain this particular human behavior in some logical manner...humans think that putting up the tree and hanging those things is a fun event. It's a ritual for a lot of them. You're probably thinking to yourself, "Wait! They have it all wrong—the fun part is knocking off the shiny things and chasing them across the floor!" Of course that's true, so there's really no explanation for why humans do what they do with the Christmas tree ritual. And even weirder, once the shiny things are hung, they don't want them moved for weeks! I know, I know, the thought of having a tree full of shiny things and never touching them is downright ghastly. Sometimes I really do wonder why we bother associating with humans. They must put some kind of drug in our kibble or something.

But the Christmas tree ritual gets worse. When they do finally take off the shiny things, they do it carefully and put them neatly away in a box and don't touch them for the rest of the year. Please understand, this is as painful for me to write as it is for you to read. Then, instead of leaving the tree for us cats to climb all over, they get rid of it. After they take all the shiny things off they call the tree a "fire hazard." Apparently fire hazards are not meant to be fun climbing toys. I don't get it, either.

But don't let the whole human Christmas tree ritual get you down too much. Those shiny things

Advice From One Cat to Another

don't make the best toys anyhow. If you give 'em a good bat across the room, they break into a bunch of sharp pieces and if you step on them you might cut yourself. And I hope your humans are smart enough not to hang those stringy, shiny tinsel things on the tree—they're really dangerous for us cats. If we eat them it might kill us. At the very least it'll be a very traumatic trip to the emergency vet clinic. Maybe someday humans will wise up and create a cat-friendly Christmas tree—one that we can climb on all we want and that has shiny things that don't break when rolled across the floor. Until that unlikely day, if you really, really can't resist messing with the human's tree, I recommend you do it in the middle of the night when they're sleeping. If you break anything, pretend you had nothing to do with it. You know the routine.

Advice From One Cat to Another

Shunning the Hunt

Dear Sparkle,
My humans are really lame. I love to go out and hunt for snacks—you know, birds, mice, an occasional squirrel (although squirrels are more of a meal). The usual. I already know I can't expect my humans to eat my catch. But I didn't want to leave them totally out of the loop, so I figured I'd bring home live prey every now and again so they could at least enjoy the catch-and-release game. The only problem is they hate it! I bring back a little mouse and let it go running on the kitchen floor and they freak out! They scream and then they yell at me to go get it—what's up with that? I brought the thing home for *them* to play with! Seriously, are humans really that stupid?
Signed,
Confounded

Dear Confounded,
I hate to tell you this, but yes, humans really are that stupid. Now, this is just my opinion, mind you, but I think it comes from eating too much fast food. I'm not talking about the nutritional value of fast food, or the lack thereof (although I hear my fitness freak human discussing that topic constantly)—it has to do with the form the fast food comes in. In other words, it's completely preformed and packaged and bears no resemblance to the cow or chicken it came from (or potato or wheat, for that matter).

Dear Sparkle

Humans have a hard time connecting meat to something that was once living and breathing. In fact the thought kind of grosses a lot of them out, which is really dumb. Most humans live in some sort of weird fantasyland, where they never see a whole animal before they eat it. Usually they just see the parts, and usually those parts are already prepared too because "who has time to cook anymore?" (I've heard humans say that more than once.) In fact, humans have gotten so far away from the food chain that they think that "playing with your food" means taking a fork and pushing the peas under the mashed potatoes. Give me a break!

What would humans do if suddenly all the restaurants and markets went away and they had to fend for themselves? Wouldn't that be an ugly sight! It kind of makes you want to bring live prey home to train them just in case, doesn't it? But unfortunately, when it comes to hunting most humans are pretty much untrainable. They don't understand the game of the hunt at all. You're lucky your humans aren't the type who chase after the mice so they can catch them and set them free—it's really a bummer after you've gone through all the effort of catching something only to have someone take it away from you. Your humans at least just want you to have it. So to keep the peace, you might as well do just that—play with the creatures you catch on your own. Sure, you can take one inside every so often and do the catch-and-release game just to show your humans what they're missing. But I doubt they'll get it. If they don't like protracted hunting of small game, it's their loss.

Advice From One Cat to Another

Advice From One Cat to Another

Cat Toy Alternatives

Dear Sparkle,
I am just seven months old, but I am big for my age. I've recently found a new home with a family of humans and since I look like I'm practically grown up they think that I don't need any cat toys. They bought me one dumb catnip mouse that doesn't even have much of a scent. Clearly this is unacceptable, but what can I do? It's not like I can just dash over to the pet store myself and load up on some cool toys. I'm going to have to make do with what's around here. Do you have any suggestions for which human items make the best cat toys?
Signed,
Vaguely Annoyed

Dear Annoyed,
Although it was very nice of your humans to give you a home, they really seem pretty clueless when it comes to cats. Sure, kittens love to play (and at seven months you're definitely still a kitten), but so do grown up cats. Somalis are playful all their lives—that's one of the reasons my human got me. She didn't want some boring "doorstop of a cat" (her words, not mine). So my home is loaded with cat toys. Of course, my human has the bad habit of getting the wrong cat toys, but that's another problem altogether, and certainly a better one than yours. I mean, even the wrong toys are better than no toys at all.

Dear Sparkle

Like many cats before you who have suffered through the same dilemma, you will just have to play with whatever you can find lying around the house. The great thing is that cats' imaginations are far more fanciful than humans' are, so there is probably a wealth of potential toys that your humans may consider mere "junk." In fact, some of the best places for you to start looking for makeshift cat toys are the various trashcans around the house. If there's an office, the trash is probably filled with crumbled up papers you can dig out and bat around. Crumbled papers make really fascinating sounds, especially on wood floors. You might also find some small cardboard containers in the office trash or in the bathroom trashcan (those cardboard tubes in the bathroom trash will give you some good action). Small, empty plastic bottles also make fun play toys.

The best trash can, in case you haven't figured this out already, is the one in the kitchen because not only will you find things to use as toys, you can also occasionally grab a handy snack or two. Some humans know about this cat treasure trove and have taken measures to keep us out of it. I bet your humans are not yet aware of how awesome kitchen trash is, so take advantage of their ignorance—it probably won't last very long. Do, however, stay away from anything really stinky, like old cleaning rags. They're toxic—but then, they smell so bad you will probably not want to touch them anyhow.

Of course, the trash isn't the only place to find great toys. Maybe there are some knickknacks sitting on tables or mantelpieces that are just waiting

Advice From One Cat to Another

to be knocked to the floor and batted around. Are there children in your family? They usually have loads of stuff that cats love—small, plush animals to kill, action figures to carry in your mouth, doll accessories to knock around until they disappear under the dresser.

Perhaps the best item of all, however, isn't even a kid toy or a knickknack or even trash. It's those long plastic things that humans call "pens." Pens are a joy to play with and inevitably they roll under the couch or somewhere else that's equally inaccessible to humans. I heard of one cat that used to keep his humans virtually penless—they'd have to move all the furniture in the living room if they wanted to write any notes. Half the fun was watching the humans hunt for the pens! Which is another source of amusement—watching the humans react after you turn some boring object of theirs into a fun toy. The curious thing is that, instead of being grateful for the insight, they usually get kind of annoyed. And since you signed your letter "vaguely annoyed," I think it's only poetic justice that your return the favor.

Dear Sparkle

2
Other Cats & Miscellaneous Creatures

Some cats are solitary in nature and others are more social. The one thing we all have in common is that we hate change. And we really hate change when it involves the introduction of a new creature into our lives, whether it's another cat or another species altogether. And sometimes the problem isn't even a new roommate—it's the presence of any creature, indoors or out, that doesn't belong on our turf. When a cat's territory is disturbed, it's not a laughing matter. That's why many cats come crying to me.

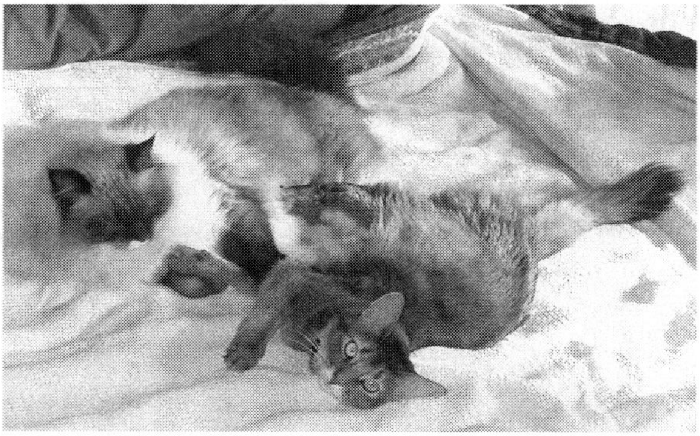

Advice From One Cat to Another

Brother from Another Mother

Dear Sparkle,
We are a pair of cats who are living happily with a great human. We get roasted chicken and catnip as treats on a regular basis. Now our human tells us that she is bringing us home a "new little brother" in a few weeks. Neither of us quite understand what she means by this—we are not related to each other to begin with so we're not sure how she could be bringing home a kitten related to both of us. But apparently that's what she says she is doing. Whether or not this new kitty is an actual relative, we are concerned—does this mean there will be less treats for us? What happens if we don't like this new kitten? Should we beat him up if he refuses to acknowledge our superiority? We're really not sure what to make of this whole situation.
Signed,
Concerned Kitties

Dear Concerned Kitties,
Humans are a quirky bunch. They bring home cats you've never seen before in your life and insist that they are your new "brother" or "sister." They're really into this strange world of make-believe when it comes to relatives. We cats choose who we want to be close to, and being a brother, sister, aunt or second cousin isn't an important consideration. For some reason, humans think it is, and I really don't get it, because I've heard humans complain very

Dear Sparkle

loudly about other humans they are related to. In any case, it makes me glad I'm a cat. Life is way less complicated for us.

Which brings us to what is going on in your household—your human is bringing home a kitten and you are worried you may not like him. This is a valid concern, believe me. A new cat, whether he is young or full grown, is always a disruption to a peaceful home. So I hope your human is smart enough to confine the new kitten to a room all his own for a while, with his own food, water and litter box. Just knowing that the kitten is there is disruptive enough, even without seeing him. I do recommend checking out the empty carrier he arrived in, to see how he smells (you may find this offensive at first, but you know what? I've heard of cats who hated each other's smells at first who later on became close friends).

Once the kitten has settled in for a few days, your human will probably put some time aside to make an introduction. While this may be traumatic, there is a good side to this—instead of less treats, you might wind up getting *more*! That's because your human will want you to associate the kitten with good things, so she will probably give you treats if you don't just charge ahead and beat up the kitten first thing. If you behave yourselves, you'll probably get a treat when the introductory session is over too. In fact, I'd suggest that even if you don't find the kitten all that distasteful, hold back on your approval just so your human has to arrange more supervised meetings, accompanied by more treats and, perhaps, toys.

Dear Sparkle

After a few meetings, if everything goes well, the kitten will probably be allowed full run of the house and your human will probably stop watching you all so closely. If you want to make sure the kit-ten acknowledges your superiority as the Cats Who Were There First, this is a good time to bop him on the nose. Because kittens are irreverent little creatures, a good slap or two is often warranted. Just avoid doing it in front of the human, who will probably freak out. No use causing humans stress over routine cat hierarchy maintenance, you know. I'm sure you guys will all come to a mutual understanding eventually.

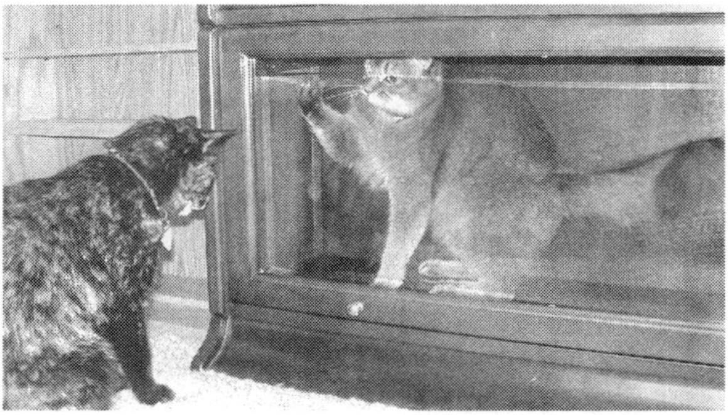

Advice From One Cat to Another

Taunting Tom Trouble

Dear Sparkle,
I used to be a common alley cat, but when my humans adopted me from the shelter, they decided I should stay indoors. It's okay. I've adjusted. I mean, 3 squares a day is certainly better than chasing after scrawny little mice that are barely a mouthful. Plus I've got a huge, floor-to-ceiling cat tree—with sisal! But here's the problem: I spend a good portion of the day sitting by the window and checking out things on the outside—you know, just to make sure no one's messing with my yard. And you know what...someone *is* messing with my yard! It's a big yellow tom, and he won't go away! He stares at me intently and then goes over and sprays on the bushes. The jerk knows I can't do a thing about it, and I'm infuriated! I howl at him through the window. A couple of times I totally lost control and started throwing myself against the windowpane. Like I said, I'm happy indoors, but this Tom has gotta go. Any suggestions?
Signed,
Furious Beyond Meows

Dear Furious,
I really can't blame you for being furious. It must be frustrating, watching that Tom mess with your turf. For all its great benefits—the regular meals, cat trees, etc.—living indoors does have a few drawbacks, and this is one of them. It's especially hard on

Dear Sparkle

guys like you who are used to being out of doors and dealing with unruly visitors in claw-to-claw combat. Unfortunately, there's really nothing you can do to send this Tom packing. At least not on your own. To get rid of him you'll have to enlist the help of lesser beings—in other words, your humans.

Since your humans can go outside and you can't, it is up to them to get rid of that Tom. I can't believe they haven't done something about it already—most of the humans I know detest the acrid smell of male cat spray. And they must see how unhappy you are. You are making your displeasure known while they are around, aren't you? If not, you are wasting your energy. Remember, when you want results, act out in the presence of an audience. Granted, it doesn't always get you the outcome you want, but in this case, I think that carrying on about the Tom in their presence will help your cause.

There are a number of effective ways to make Toms leave your turf alone. Hopefully your humans aren't too dense, because there are also some ways that aren't particularly effective. The many cat repellants on the market—the ones that supposedly smell bad to cats—generally don't work all that well. If they want to try the scent route, they could save a lot of money by just using natural remedies, such as sprinkling cayenne pepper around the house, or vinegar, or ground-up orange peels. But like I said, at best these items will just keep the Tom away temporarily. Eventually he'll be back, eager to taunt you once again. Those repellents need constant reapplication, especially in wet weather. Another thing your humans could consider would

Advice From One Cat to Another

be to replace their lawn and landscaping with a rock garden—those sharp stones play havoc with tender kitty feet. But as much as they swear their devotion to you, I doubt they'll go that far to get rid of this unwelcome visitor. There is a certain kind of plant called a coleus canina that has a scent that both dogs and cats dislike—maybe they could at least add a few of them to the yard.

The most effective way I've heard of to get rid of a wayward Tom, however—and I think you'll like this solution quite a bit—is a device that blasts unwelcome animal visitors with water. Your humans can probably find it at the local pet store or on the web. They set it up in the yard and the motion sensor detects when the Tom is paying a visit. Once he is spotted, he gets a surprise drenching, which I guarantee will send him running! I doubt he'll get caught more than a couple of times before he'll be gone for good. And since you enjoy looking out the window, you'll get a front row view of his humiliation. Once this thing is installed, no stray cat will dare invade your turf.

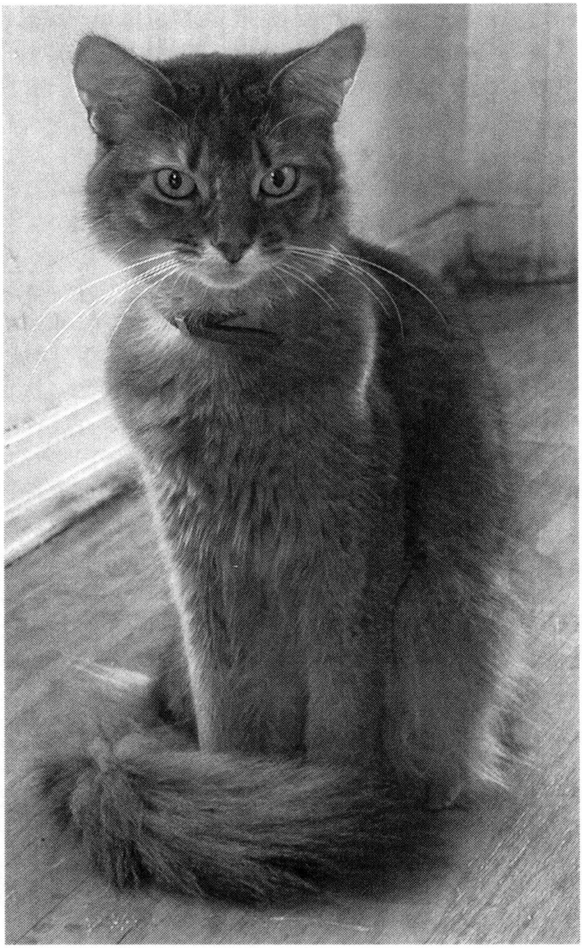

Advice From One Cat to Another

Human Kitten?

Dear Sparkle,
The weirdest thing is going on in my home right now! The humans just brought home this really strange little creature and they are making the biggest deal out of it. I actually think it's kind of ugly—it doesn't have any fur and it's kind of noisy at times. It sort of looks like an unfinished, miniature human. Whatever it is, it's totally helpless and the humans have to do everything for it. They even have a whole room devoted to this thing. Even though, like I said, it isn't the most attractive creature in the world it seems okay. I mean, at least it's not another cat! What do I do about this creature? Should I make friends with it? It's not going to steal my food, is it?
Signed,
Mystified

Dear Mystified,
When you said that this creature looks like an unfinished, miniature human, you were actually right on the mark because that's exactly what it is! It's the human version of a kitten, called a "baby." Babies actually aren't as fun as kittens because they are so helpless for such a long time. It takes them many months to mature enough to be playful, and even then you had better hope your humans train it well—unfortunately babies grow in size faster than their ability to know the difference between "playful" and "hurtful" when it comes to us kitties.

Dear Sparkle

But you won't have to deal with an overactive, untrained baby for a while yet. Right now your biggest concern is making sure that your humans don't totally neglect you in favor of the baby. If they do, they don't mean to—I'm sure your mother neglected her humans when she had you and your brothers and sisters. The best thing you can do right now is just be there—hang around where ever the humans are, sit next to them if you want and generally be present. They probably won't be feeling terribly playful a lot of the time. Humans don't have as natural a parenting instinct as cats and other creatures do, so they are usually pretty stressed out when they have a new baby to deal with. You'll have to cope with that the best you can.

Chances are you won't get much access to the baby's room, which is really a pity. Babies are warm so they're nice to sleep with, and the tops of their bottles make fun toys to bat around. But it's almost a given that the humans will put some sort of cover or tent over the baby's crib to keep you out, and they will not appreciate you playing hockey with any of the baby's things. If you want to get to know the baby, you'll pretty much have to do it on the humans' terms.

As far as stealing your food, that won't happen for a good, long while. When the baby starts to crawl around, the humans will probably keep an eye on it and keep it away from your food. The problem will come when they get used to it roaming around and they aren't quite as watchful. Then you might find the baby in your bowl. But if this happens, just complain loudly. Your humans will be more than happy to remove the baby from your food.

Advice From One Cat to Another

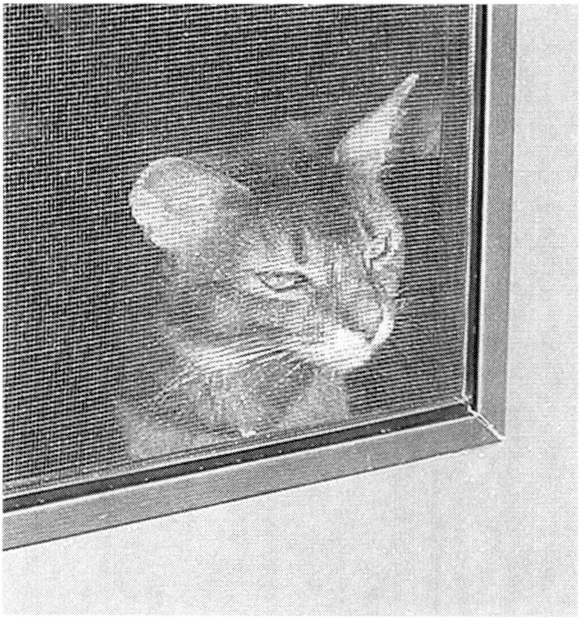

Advice From One Cat to Another

Birds on the Brain

Dear Sparkle,
I am so frustrated I am about to explode! But let me start from the beginning. I live in this big apartment complex with my human. I love looking out the window at all the goings on and I especially enjoy watching the birds. The only problem is a couple of those birds have decided to taunt me! They know that I can't get at them through the window screen, so they hang out and stare me down! It makes me crazy—I'll cling to the screen and yell at them but they just twitter at me. Grrrr! I want to teach those birds a lesson they'll never forget, but to be honest I have no desire to be an outdoor kitty. The outdoors, as far as I can tell, is a big concrete wasteland with a few strategically placed trees. So I prefer to stay indoors. Is there any way I can get at those birds without leaving the comfort of my cozy apartment?
Signed,
Royally PO'd

Dear PO'd,
When you said you didn't want to go outdoors to give those birds their well-deserved lesson, I thought at first that you were a bit of a wimp. Then you described your surroundings as mostly concrete and I could understand its lack of appeal. There is good news, however—you don't necessarily have to venture into the concrete jungle to get back at those birds. The whole secret revolves around that handy window screen.

Dear Sparkle

Window screens are actually wonderful things for us cats. We can enjoy nice breezes and outdoor views without all the dangers of the outdoor world. But even better, we can occasionally mold these screens to suit our needs. You may have noticed that when you claw at the screen, you sometimes create a few small holes. (When we do this in our home, it annoys our human to no end, but of course that doesn't stop us.) Have you ever thought about making those little claw holes just a bit bigger? How about making them big enough so that you can stick a paw through? Do you see where I'm going with this? If you make an arm-sized hole, the next time one of those birds comes flying around to annoy you, you just shoot your paw out and snatch him! Instant bird dinner. And believe me, after that, those other birds will show you a lot more respect.

If you are even luckier, you may not even have to snatch the bird—it may be stupid enough to actually fly through the hole all by itself. And once it's on your turf, it will serve as a fun play toy. Plus it will probably be too scared to figure out how to get back out again. The truth is that birds are not very bright. I mean, have you ever heard the term "bird brain"? Really, outfoxing a bird should be pretty simple for any cat. I'm sure that if you'd thought things through before dropping me a line, you would have figured out the solution on your own.

Advice From One Cat to Another

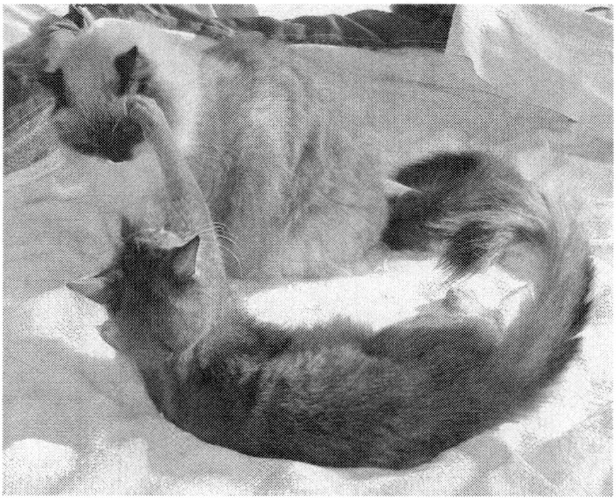

Advice From One Cat to Another

Fighting for Fun

Dear Sparkle,
My human doesn't understand me (what else is new?). I've been locked in the house all winter and I'm sick of it, and of course I've been looking for fun activities to keep busy. Well, I came up with a great pastime—wrestling with my roommate, a neutered tomcat like myself. We love it! (Well, I love it, my roommate sometimes thinks I play too rough, but that's his problem.) After a good wrestling match that leaves fur all over the rug, we often like to curl up together with my human for a light snooze. My human is completely puzzled by this and she thinks I'm being mean to my roommate. She keeps talking about trying to find us a new pastime, like the one we've got isn't good enough! How do I get her off my back?
Signed,
Good Time Aggressor

Dear GTA,
I hear you, big guy. It happens at my house all the time too. Binga and I love beating up on Boodie and my human is always telling us we're too rough. But if Boodie didn't like it she wouldn't keep on coming back for more. And, as the Beta (non-dominant) cat in our household, it is her job to take a licking (and biting and getting jumped on). So it goes with you and your roommate. Obviously playing rough has little negative impact on your relationship—you both can settle in for a nice, relaxing nap. If

Dear Sparkle

you guys really hated each other, you'd be screeching and howling and drawing blood. Humans just can't seem to grasp all this, but as you know they are a little soft in the head. I mean, what does this say about them? Apparently they can't tell the difference between hard play and fighting and when they get upset, they can't make up with the person they disagreed with. No wonder humans have such a hard time getting along with each other.

But anyhow, onto your problem. As long as your human sees your wrestling matches, it will upset her, so your best idea would be to do it when she isn't around. If you keep wrestling in front of her, she may start doing dumb things like trying to distract you with toys or squirt you with a spray bottle (yecch!). If she tries any of this, I recommend that you do your best to ignore her. Here's the reason why: she may eventually resort to distracting you with treats. Now, if she starts doing that, cool! That is definitely a good distraction, and worth abandoning the wrestling match without proving your Alpha cat manliness. In any case, once spring arrives, your human will probably start letting you out again so you can keep an eye out for real intruders, catch the occasional field mouse and just generally enjoy the good life. Maybe if you're lucky your human will be bright enough to at least figure this out and start letting you out a bit early. After all, what are fur coats for?

Advice From One Cat to Another

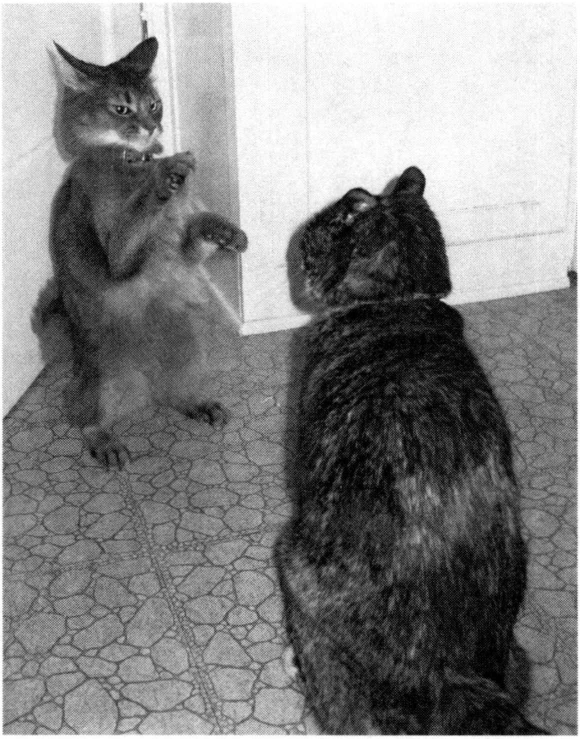

Advice From One Cat to Another

Boss or Not?

Dear Sparkle,
For the past five years, I've been the only cat living with my human. But then a couple of weeks ago she did the unthinkable—she brought home a kitten! I'm totally disgusted. My human keeps going out of her way to make sure we both get equal amounts of attention and frankly it's enough to make me puke. What's worse than my human's inane behavior, however, is that this kitten is a little snot! He thinks he's God's gift to humans and does everything he can to get more food and attention than me. So I did the logical thing—I whapped him one to put him in his place. But you know what the little jerk did? He whapped me back! The nerve! What can I do to show this squirt that I'm the boss cat around here? And do you think there's a way I can get my human to take him back to where ever he came from?
Signed,
Mad Cat

Dear Mad,
I guess I'll start with the bad news first—I doubt there's anything you can do to get rid of the new kitten. No matter how violently you react to him, your human will probably try all that much harder to make you guys get along. If you're disgusted with her behavior now, imagine what that would be like! She sounds like the type of person who reads cat psychology books, so she'd probably lock you two

Dear Sparkle

up in separate parts of the house and bring you together for short periods of recreation until you both were nice enough to each other to be allowed full reign of the house. So if you want to get locked up in a room for weeks or months, go ahead and behave badly. Just thought I'd warn you.

Other manipulations probably won't help either. You could try acting depressed—mope around, don't eat your dinner, stuff like that. It will get you extra attention from your human, and she'll probably bring home all sorts of great treats, but to make this ploy really work, you'd have to turn your nose up at all the good stuff, too. Let's face it, the depression act is really no fun. Save it for when you're really ill.

The bottom line is that your human is not going to be much use in this situation. As you already know, her efforts to "help" are laughable. This is going to be purely between you and the squirt. If you're stuck having him around—and that's probably the case—you really do need to make him realize that you are the boss cat. The direct approach—hissing and hitting—apparently doesn't impress him. So you've got to get sneaky. Attack him when he's not paying attention. This is pretty easy to do, as kittens tend to be oblivious to anything that isn't a toy. Sneak up from behind and give the "killing bite"—leap on his back, wrap your front paws around him and bite him on the neck, hard. You're not going to kill him, of course, or even draw blood—just surprise him and make him cry "uncle!" Then leap off him and attend to other business. Do this frequently. If it seems like he's going to try to fight back after you've jumped off him, give him a couple of good kicks with your hind legs and an extra bite. Yes, this is playing dirty, but that's the only way to handle an uppity little cat. Also, don't do this while your human's around. It will only distress her and she will try to intervene. Humans really don't understand the whole cat hierarchy thing. Do all your dirty work when she's not around.

Eventually the kitten will realize that you're bigger than he is and that maybe you're being kind by not doing him any serious damage. After that you should be able to come to some sort of agreement. But make sure you jump him now and again, just to keep him on his toes. Doing it from a high perch is especially effective. These tactics should work, at least until the kitten grows up. If he turns out to be bigger than you, you may have another problem to deal with.

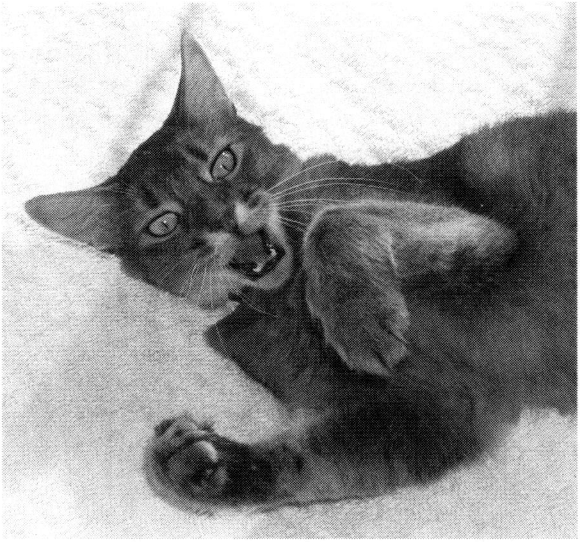

Advice From One Cat to Another

Wrong-Way Aggression

Dear Sparkle,
Something really upsetting just happened! Me and my roommate—a longhaired tabby who looks quite a bit like me—were looking out the window into the backyard. It's one of our favorite things to do because there's a bird feeder out there, and lots of birds come and hang out. But earlier this afternoon, all the birds suddenly flew off and this huge gray and white tomcat came stalking through our yard! That was disturbing enough—both me and my roommate fluffed up—but then my roommate turned around and attacked ME! It was like he thought *I* was the intruder. He chased me into the laundry room and cornered me behind the washing machine. I was stuck there for hours, waiting for him to leave. Now I'm scared to be around him. We were really great friends, but he's acting like I'm a stranger he's never seen before. What can I do?
Signed,
Freaked Out & Fluffed Out

Dear Freaked & Fluffed,
I doubt this will make you feel any better, but your roommate is suffering from a classic case of something humans call "redirected aggression." In other words, the incident with the tom upset him so much that he just had to attack someone, anyone and you just happened to be the nearest target. But it's really pointless for me to go into definitions and expla-

Dear Sparkle

nations. I imagine that at the moment you couldn't care less about why your roommate attacked you, or what his behavior is called. Humans, on the other hand, are fascinated by such things. I heard a saying once which surprisingly came from a human, not a cat. It had something to do with having "more brains than sense." That's what it should say after the word "human" in those dictionary books they love to read so much, and that we love to sit on so much.

In any case, you're more concerned about action than analyzing. You want to know what you can do about this terrible situation. I do want to say that you did the right thing by running away and hiding. A cat who is in the throes of redirected aggression has pretty much lost his head. Trying to fight back is only going to make the problem worse. And there is nothing you or your human can do to calm down a cat in this state. The best thing you can do is put distance between yourself and your aggressive roommate until he calms down. How long is this going to take? It's unpredictable, really. You could wake up the next morning to find that he's back to his normal self. Or he could treat you like the worst type of intruder indefinitely. I do want you to know that however long he behaves like a wildcat, it's not your fault. As long as you do nothing to provoke him and keep a low profile, you are not adding to the problem. In fact, that's really all you can do for now—nothing.

What I'd really like to know is where is your human while all this has been going on? Along with providing hand-delivered gourmet meals, humans are supposed to deal with problems like this one.

Advice From One Cat to Another

Your human should be keeping you two separate so you don't wind up stuck behind a washing machine for hours. And if your roommate continues acting nasty, your human should be making sure you are safe and slowly reintroducing the two of you bit by bit. It's no fun having a battlefield as a home, and it's really the human's responsibility to take care of situations like this one. If your human is ignoring the problem or being neglectful, I personally think that a bit of redirected aggression in his or her direction is in order.

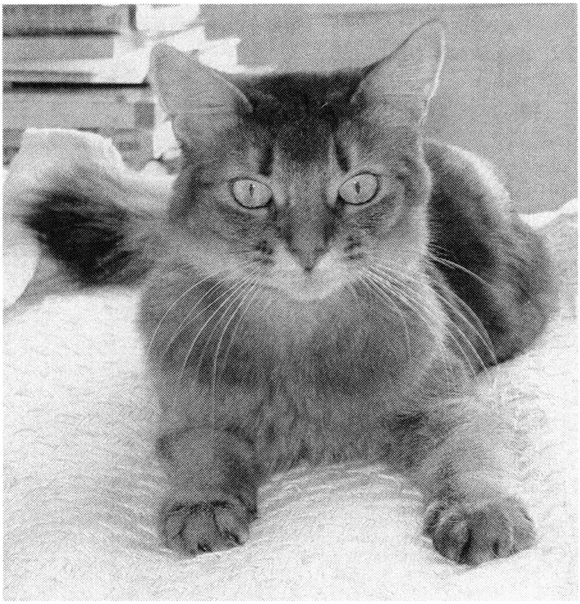

Advice From One Cat to Another

Ferret Frustration

Dear Sparkle,
Okay, now I've seen everything! My humans are big "animal people" and they're always bringing home some creature—I have to share this house with a hermit crab, a couple of frogs and a dog (luckily, the dog is about my size and is easily dominated). But just the other day they brought home something and I have no clue what to do with it! It's long and furry with a rodent face, but it's bigger than a rat so I can't eat it. It gets into everything and that really disgusts me because my humans think that's "cute." When *I* get into things, they yell at me. As you might already suspect, they dote on this creature, which they call a "ferret," and they expect me to become great friends with it. I don't see why I should let this ferret be my friend. It's annoying, it steals attention away from my humans and worst of all, it takes all my cat toys and hides them! I've got the dog under control, and the other creatures are under glass so my exposure to them is limited (which bums me out—I'm sure they'd make tasty snacks). But this ferret—I really have no idea how to show it who's in charge around here. Any suggestions?
Signed,
Confounded

Dear Confounded,
Poor you. Ferrets are a real handful. The good news is that they love to play and can't get enough of it.

Dear Sparkle

(And we all know that humans don't play enough, so it's actually kind of nice to have some-one around who's always ready to go.) The bad news is they just don't understand the whole hierarchy thing—whap 'em on the head and they think it's an invitation to play. So if you really want that ferret to let you be in charge, you're out of luck. It'll just laugh in your face. If this really gets on your nerves, I suppose you could give it a good smackdown every time it comes near you, and it will eventually leave you alone. But you know what? Maybe you shouldn't be so quick to dismiss this oversized, troublemaking rodent. Ferrets do have their uses. You yourself mentioned that it gets into everything. You've also mentioned that your human has some yummy looking creatures under glass. Maybe the ferret will figure out how to get these containers open so that you can dine on them. This would probably not make your humans terribly happy, but it's their fault for bringing a ferret home in the first place.

If none of this matters and you'll hate the ferret no matter what (not everyone's personalities mix well), then you can always pitch a fit every time you are near it. If you're hissing, howling and screeching every time the ferret is around, your humans will have no choice but to keep you guys apart. And there is a bit of good news—cats on the average live way longer than ferrets do. So if there is not much of an age difference between you and your annoying new roommate, rest assured that there will most likely come a day when it's no longer around. Just hope your humans aren't too quick to rush out and bring home another one!

3
Human Foibles

It is probably no surprise that this is the largest section of the book. For us cats, living with humans is a mixed bag. Sure, we get luxuries like premium cat food, cat condos, toys, a nice bed and a home to call our own. But we pay a price for this life of ease—we must deal with human idiosyncrasies. Sometimes I wonder if it's all worth it. So do a lot of other cats, which is why so many frustrated felines come to me for advice. Humans are complicated beings, and very hard to train. When I can guide a cat through a particularly tough human dilemma, I really feel like my job as an advice columnist is making a difference!

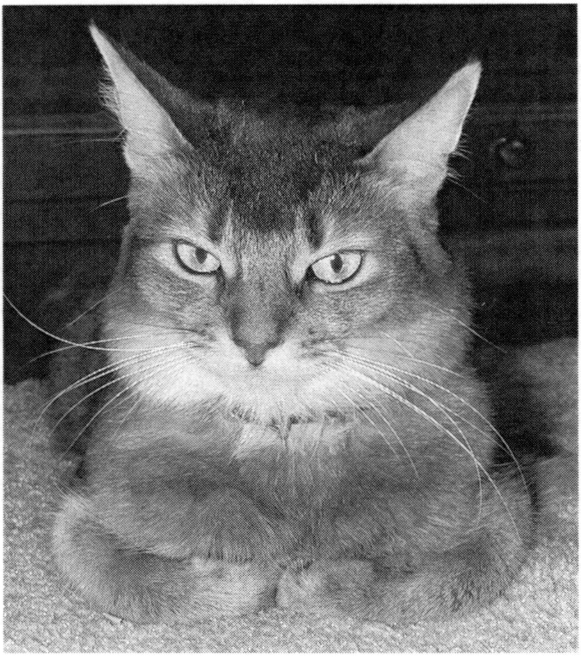

Advice From One Cat to Another

Hairball Remedy Hell

Dear Sparkle,
I'm a cat with lots and lots of fluff—not unlike your roommate Boodie. As a result I am known to have hairballs on occasion. To me they're not that big a deal—I hack them up and it's over. But my human makes an issue out of it. Every time she sees one of my hairballs, she immediately grabs me and forces this vile gel down my throat. Of course I protest when she does this and the gel winds up all over both her and myself. Needless to say, shedding season is always an unpleasant experience for me since I get this gel forced on me even more frequently than normal. Do all human punish their cats thusly for our very natural hairball hacking habit?
Signed,
Puzzled, and Rather Annoyed

Dear Puzzled and Annoyed,
The hairball issue is a common quirk among humans. It's a bit mystifying, too—for some reason, it seems like they always try to force the hairball remedy down our throats *after* we've hacked up a hairball, when it's too late to do any good. Hairball remedy is what that distasteful gel is, by the way. It's supposed to make it so that we don't hack up the fur we've licked, and pass it through our diges-tive system instead. To be honest I too am not a fan of these gels. I find the taste incredibly repul-sive. So does Boodie. Only Binga enjoys these hairball gels,

and being a domestic shorthair tortie, of course she's the one who is least likely to hack up hairballs.

So the truth—in the human's mind—is that we are not being punished at all, but being given medicine of sorts. The only problem is that it's awful tasting, pointless medicine. Maybe if you are lucky, your human will eventually discover that hairball remedies don't just come in tubes—they also come in crushable tablets and treats, which are far more palatable. There is also hairball formula cat food out there, but only the premium brands are worthwhile. You might let your human know that there *is* a way to prevent hairballs that doesn't involve shoving some vile tasting ointment on you. Maybe she could *brush* you regularly! Now, wouldn't that be a concept?

Advice From One Cat to Another

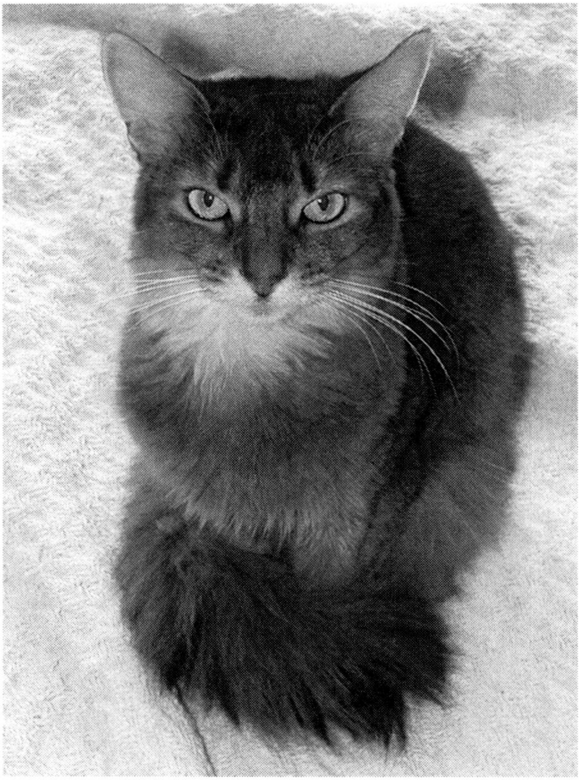

Advice From One Cat to Another

Guest Gripe

Dear Sparkle,
I have a pretty nice life with a pair of humans who rescued me from a shelter a few years ago. Whenever it's just the two of them, things are great—they play with me and give me lots of nice treats. The only problem is when they have guests come over—I hate that! I really don't care much for strangers. I mean, who knows where they've been and what they've been doing? I don't trust them so I do the only logical thing—I hide from them. That's okay when the guests only visit for a little while, say, a few hours, but sometimes they stick around for a couple of weeks! Do you have any idea what it's like, having to sneak around in your own home when you need to use the litter box? It's really no fun. So I want to know—how do I convince my humans to stop having guests over?
Signed,
Reluctant Recluse

Dear Recluse,
I am not a big fan of guests, either—they smell funny and like you said, who knows where they've been and what they've been doing? In spite of all this, I've found it next to impossible to make humans stop having guests over. It seems like it's almost a compulsion! We cats have more sense—does anyone ever see us inviting another cat over to spend the evening or—horrors!—a week or two? Of course not!

Dear Sparkle

But humans seem to need the company of other humans on occasion. It's one of their more unappealing traits, if you ask me.

But I have learned that guests do have their good points, if you are willing to come out from un-der the bed and take advantage of them. If they like cats, you can milk them for treats and playtime. Even if your humans don't allow you to beg for food, you can usually get away with it with guests. What's even more entertaining is if the guests don't like cats—then you can annoy them by climbing all over them and getting in their face. The added benefit to this is that if you irritate them enough, they won't come around anymore.

If you really can't stand the guests and you don't want to act friendly to them, there are ways to make them not want to come back. You can crawl all over their stuff and shed lots of fur. This is especially effective if your fur is a radically different shade from the guests' things—like, if you're white and they wear lots of black. If they aren't fazed by this, there are other ways of adorning their things with your fur—namely with a carefully placed hairball. That will make them not want to return. If they're really, really persistent then it's time to pull out the big guns and use their bags as your litter box (hey, it's probably closer than your regular litter box is, right?). As both humans and cats know, the smell of cat urine is extremely enduring and very hard to get rid of. Those pesky guests, however, will be very easy to get rid of once you've tried out this tactic. And I can almost guarantee they won't be coming back. This last trick will probably make your hu-

Advice From One Cat to Another

mans mad at you for a few days, but if you really, really hate having guests over, it's worth the temporary inconvenience.

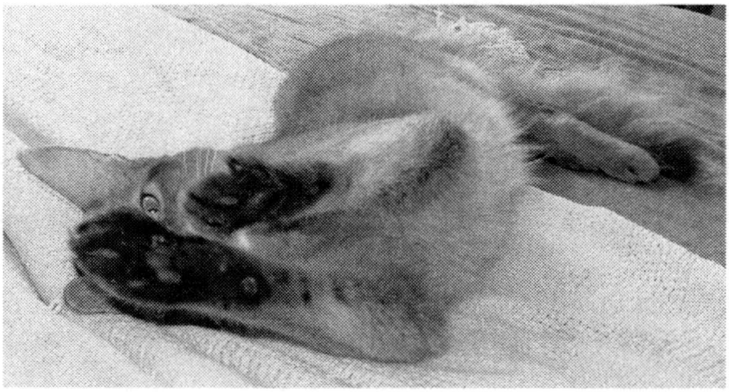

Advice From One Cat to Another

Getting Your Paw in the Door

Dear Sparkle,
I'm homeless at the moment, but I've found a neighborhood with several families who feed me. I've decided I want to live at this one house—they have a couple of dogs (yuck), but the husband is really nice and he goes out of his way to buy cat food for me. The wife thinks they don't need a cat (ha!) and tries to chase me away but I just ignore her when she starts telling me to leave. I tried getting into the house one night by climbing on the window screen in the bedroom and creating a racket, but they wouldn't let me in. How do I get into the house and make these people realize that I've decided to stay?
Signed,
Dirty but Determined

Dear Dirty,
Hm. Judging from what you've decided to call yourself, I'd say take a tongue bath first before trying anything else. Otherwise, once you get inside you may find yourself subjected to a bath *with water*, and you know that's no fun!

Anyhow, onto your dilemma...people are funny things, aren't they? First they feed you, and then they pretend they have no idea why you've decided to come live with them. The solution here is twofold—in addition to getting into the house, you should really try to ingratiate yourself with the wife. Instead

Dear Sparkle

of acting snotty when she tries to shoo you off, look up at her with big, plaintive eyes and talk to her in soft tones. Try rubbing up against her legs. If she doesn't seem to like that, then just hang out near her when she's outside, as if you enjoy being in her presence. Granted, some of this may seem rather manipulative, but hey, we're cats! Manipulation is our middle name.

As for getting into the house—what kind of cat are you that you even need to ask? This should be instinctive. Have you checked all around the place to see if there's anywhere to sneak in? People usually have their homes secure enough to keep out other, unwanted people, but they don't realize that a cat can get into some really miniscule holes. It's best to do your snooping when no one is home—that way, if you get in, you can wander around to your heart's content and get to know your new home before you're actually invited to stay. Some key areas to look are under the house and around those window screens—sometimes, if the window is open, you can pull a screen open and climb in.

The next step is what I fondly refer to as "barging right in"—wait until the people come home from the store and their arms are loaded with bags. The moment the door is open, rush right in under their feet—they won't have any free hands to stop you. Once you're inside, immediately make yourself at home in the kitchen and ask to be fed. If, for some reason, the people seem upset that you're inside, don't let them grab you—dash off to another room. Throw yourself on the floor and roll around on your back. Show them how much you love it there. Keep

Advice From One Cat to Another

repeating this process from room to room until the people give up and feed you. If you manage to get thrown out (and I imagine this will happen to you the first couple of times), keep barging right in whenever you get the opportunity. Eventually this couple will realize that they're stuck with you and let you stay.

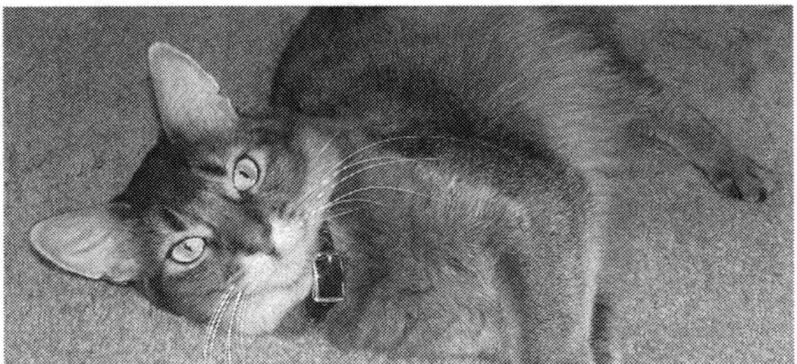

Advice From One Cat to Another

Kissing Conundrum

Dear Sparkle,
What can I do about my human—she's really annoying! She's always picking me up and kissing me and I hate it! She never even asks for permission—there I am, wandering around the house, minding my own business when out of nowhere she swoops down and grabs me and starts kissing me on the head. Even worse is when I'm sleeping—I'm dreaming of catching a big, fat rat and the next thing I know, she's sneaking up on me and pushing her lips into my fur. Now, don't get me wrong. She's really okay for a human. She serves excellent food (that chunky gourmet stuff you're always talking about), plus I get treats whenever I ask for them (well, usually). But what's with this kissing business and how do I make it stop?
Signed,
Exasperated

Dear Exasperated,
Oh, the kissing thing—that really is one irritating human habit, isn't it? I'm not quite sure how the human kissing thing originated, but I have some ideas. You know how we cats like rubbing our faces against things so that we mark them with our scent? I bet that kissing has the same function for humans—they probably have some sort of glands in their lips and when they kiss you, they're marking you as their possession. Isn't that funny? As if *we*

Dear Sparkle

belong to *them*! I know that this is an absolutely ludicrous assumption, but that is just the way humans see things. You know what's really weird, though? Some cats actually *like* to be kissed. If you ask me, I think there's something strange about cats who enjoy having human lips forced on them. Yeech. But let's look at your dilemma. A kiss now and again is an acceptable quirk, one of those annoyances that we cats must endure as a tradeoff for the creature comforts we get from living with these curious beings. But it seems to me like your human is rather obsessive about the kissing thing, so you will have to train her to curtail her bad habit.

As you have probably already discovered, scowling to show your displeasure has little effect on humans (for some reason they seem to think it's "cute"), so you need to be a little more obvious. If she's holding you while forcing herself on you, struggle and whine. Because cats are so flexible, it is generally pretty easy to slip out of the most te-nacious human grasp. Then go somewhere where she can't get at you—under the bed or behind the couch are always good choices.

Same thing if she wakes you up from a blissful slumber—leave and take your nap somewhere else, somewhere she won't fit. If she is really persistent about disturbing your sleep and you don't want to be stuck crawling under the bed all the time, then pick a high place. The top of the refrigerator is almost always a good choice—most female humans aren't tall enough to kiss you if you're up there. She can only reach up and pet you, which of course is what she should be doing anyway instead of kiss-

Advice From One Cat to Another

ing. Or if you're handy, open up a cupboard and nap there. Napping in the cupboard is always fun because the first few times you do it, the humans can't find you and they start freaking out. It is really amusing to listen to them panic while you're all cozy and hidden.

If you've tried everything and your human continues to persist in her bad kissing habits, try this tip I learned from my roommate Binga: bite her on the nose. Not too hard, just hard enough so she says, "Ouch!" and lets go of you, but not hard enough to make her scream. You don't really want to hurt her, after all. Pretend like biting her nose is a display of affection. If she thinks you're doing it because you like her, she can't get too mad. But after you've bitten her nose a few times, she will be a lot more cautious about putting her lips near your head, believe me.

Now if we could only train our humans to head-butt…but I'm sure that's beyond their grasp.

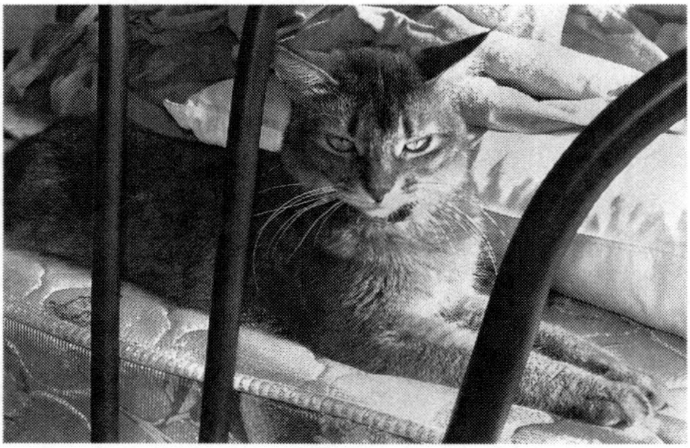

Advice From One Cat to Another

Open Door Policy

Dear Sparkle,
My humans are always complaining about what they refer to as my "barging in." What this means is that they hate it when I open doors and let myself into rooms where I am apparently not wanted. Isn't this kind of presumptuous of them? I mean, I live here—do they expect me to confine myself to certain areas of the house and avoid others? These humans are really poor roommates, if you ask me—when they brought me home they never said anything about restrictions! In fact they should be thrilled with me for opening the doors as cleverly as I do—my other feline roommate, who is a lot fluffier but quite a bit dumber, couldn't open a door to save her life! Do you think I should dump this place and go find somewhere else to live that is a bit more amenable to my presence?
Signed,
Displeased

Dear Displeased,
It certainly sounds like your humans are a bit heavy on the house rules. Either that or they're not up on cat etiquette. Any human with a bit of savvy should understand that cats go where ever they want in the house, period. That includes rooms with shut doors—bathrooms, guest rooms, closets and the like. If we can manage to get the door open, there is no reason for us to stay out. In general humans

Dear Sparkle

hate it the most when you "barge" into the bathroom while they're in it. I don't know what the big deal is about that—they certainly don't take our feelings into consideration when *we're* busy in the litter box. In fact my human will periodically sit and actually *watch* us cats when we're in there! She says she needs to do this to check on our health, but I think it is rather nervy. So as you can see, you are not alone in your complaint. It is just another case of bad human behavior. Like, what else is new?

I do want to say that judging by your cleverness and use of multi-syllable words, you are quite an intelligent kitty. But even the smartest cats can't just pack up and move and expect to find a home that is, as you say, more "amenable." In fact, usually the opposite happens—a runaway cat might not even find a new home at all and could wind up living on the streets and eating out of garbage cans. (Admittedly, I know some cats who think garbage cans are heavenly, but I get the feeling you are not one of them.) And if a new set of humans does take you in, there's no telling what you're going to get. They could be nice but uninformed—like, they'll give you that horrible, cheap canned food from the supermarket or never buy you cat toys. Or they could be downright awful, the kind of people who will ship you off to the pound the moment you have an "accident" or put a few claw marks on their couch. It's a dangerous world out there.

To be honest, I don't see that your humans are all that bad, just a little rigid. You don't say that they are doing anything about your "barging in" except complaining about it. And since when has com-

Advice From One Cat to Another

plaining ever gotten in the way of a cat doing exactly what he or she wants to do? Just ignore them and go wherever you want to go. Maybe they'll even get tired of complaining and pipe down after a while. As I'm sure you already know, persistence always wins out.

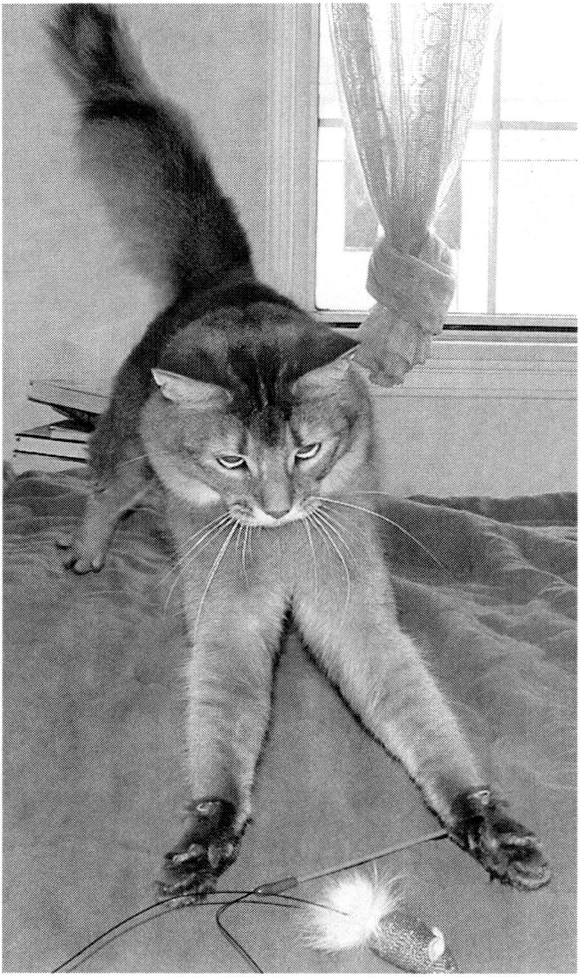

Advice From One Cat to Another

Dogged Drivel

Dear Sparkle,
I am an American Shorthair and my human and I have gotten along great for all the years she's owned me. Before she took me in, I was a barn cat and now I get treats, lots of petting and she even lets me curl up on her head when she's sleeping in that big bed. To pay her back, I humor her by coming when she calls, or patting her leg. But now she's telling people I'm a "trained" cat, and that I'm just like a dog. This is undignified! I've tried everything from ignoring her, glaring, and even not coming in to sleep on the bed at night. But nothing works. What should I do to stop my human from calling me a dog of a cat?
Signed,
Embarrassed House Cat

Dear Embarrassed,
Isn't that just like a human? They say insulting things about you, and then act as if they don't understand why you are offended. Granted, they are dense beings, but even the most thick-skulled human must realize that likening a cat to a dog is akin to declaring war with the whole feline species! Your human needs to stop doing this, and fast. It is clear that her rude behavior is giving you a complex.

Like many cats before you, you are attempting to solve the problem through passive-aggressive means. As I said, humans are dense and they

Dear Sparkle

usually aren't able to connect the dots—yours just doesn't see the relationship between your ignoring her and refusing to come to bed with her "dog" remarks. You must use direct means to get her to stop. So just think logically—she is saying you are like a dog. What would make her stop? If you halted any behavior that could be compared to the way a dog acts. Do you ever perform any of your so-called "tricks" when your human has friends over? If so, then she probably enjoys showing off just how much like a dog you are. So next time she starts bragging, just refuse to play. Don't come when she calls. Don't do anything "cute." In fact, if there's anything breakable around, knock it over while your human is bragging about how great a "dog" you are. I mean, isn't breaking things supposed to be "cat" behavior? So show off just how much of a cat you really are.

Now, here comes the best part—*this* is the time to pull out the passive-aggressiveness! Whenever no one is around, you can do all the tricks you want—come any time she calls, pat her on the leg, even sit up and beg or anything else. But do none of these things around anyone but your human. If no one else sees all these great tricks you are supposedly doing, then no one will believe what your human says and she will have to shut up with the "dog" comments. She has embarrassed you long enough—it's time you turned the embarrassment back onto her. If you follow my advice, trust me, she will never call you a dog again!

Advice From One Cat to Another

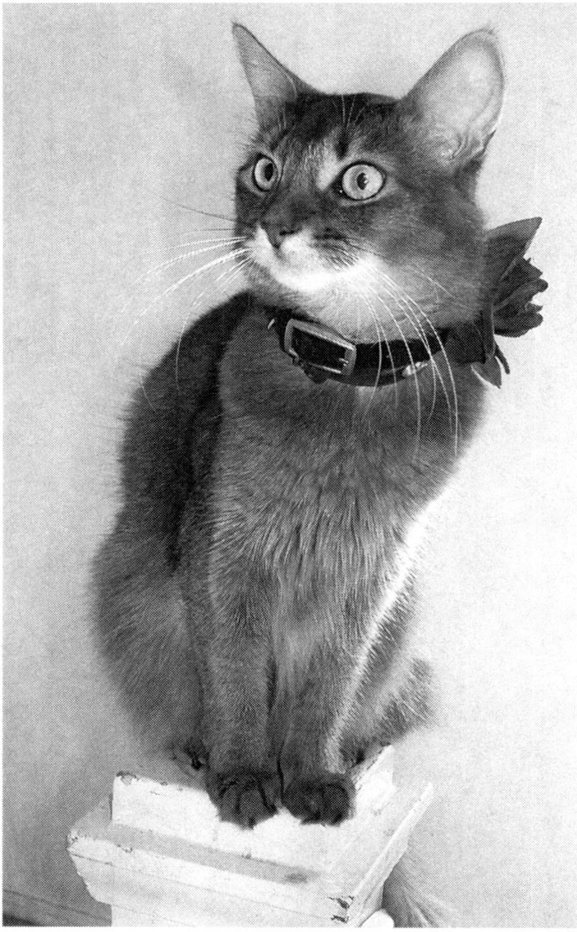

Advice From One Cat to Another

Collar Conflict

Dear Sparkle,
I'm six months old and until recently I was living outside and having lots of fun visiting a lot of different homes and getting fed by lots of different humans. Well, one family of humans decided this meant I was "homeless" (which is weird—it was more like I had a half dozen homes) and they invited me to stay with them. Since they're very nice I thought living with them would be a good idea, but I'm not so sure at the moment. The female human came home the other day with this noose-like thing with a shiny metal object attached, and she stuck it around my neck. What an awful experience—I thought I was being strangled! I did somersaults trying to get the thing off. I finally slipped it over my head and I hid under the bed for the rest of the night to show my displeasure. From what I gather, this noose is called a "collar" and they're gonna try to stick it on me again. How can I keep them from torturing me like this?
Signed,
Messed With and Mad

Dear Messed With,
I hear you about the collar thing. I don't like collars either. In fact, I did a few somersaults of my own the first time my human stuck one on me. Only humans would think of putting collars on cats—I mean, look at them! They're always putting stuff on

Dear Sparkle

their own bodies. The clothes I can kind of understand—they need something to cover up with since they don't have fur. But their passion for things like bracelets, necklaces and rings is really beyond me. Humans seem to think that collars make us look more attractive. I have to disagree—we cats look just fine without them. Embellishments like collars are pretty much pointless. Well, except for one thing: that shiny metal object you mentioned. It's a nametag that identifies you as "belonging" to the humans who put it on you. That way if you get "lost" (in other words, if you decide to wander off for a few days to see if any other humans are offering better food), someone will be able to contact your humans to come and get you.

The nametag thing is a mixed bag. It's nice to know that you won't be identified as a stray and carted off to the pound, but on the other hand, if you try begging for food from strangers, they'll assume that you're already getting fed at home and might not offer you any snacks. And it certainly is annoying to have it dangling off your neck. But the alternative isn't too great either—instead of the nametag, your humans could decide to have you "microchipped," which means a vet shoots a little computer chip between your shoulder blades, and the chip has all your identifying information. Humans say the procedure is painless, but how would they know? I don't see them lining up to get a big needle stuck between their shoulder blades. So if you insist on removing the collar every time your humans put it on you, they may just cart you off to the vet's to get chipped. If your humans are really anal retentive, they may have you chipped and

Advice From One Cat to Another

make you wear the collar and nametag, too. I don't know what to tell you, except to say that's what you get when you let humans "adopt" you.

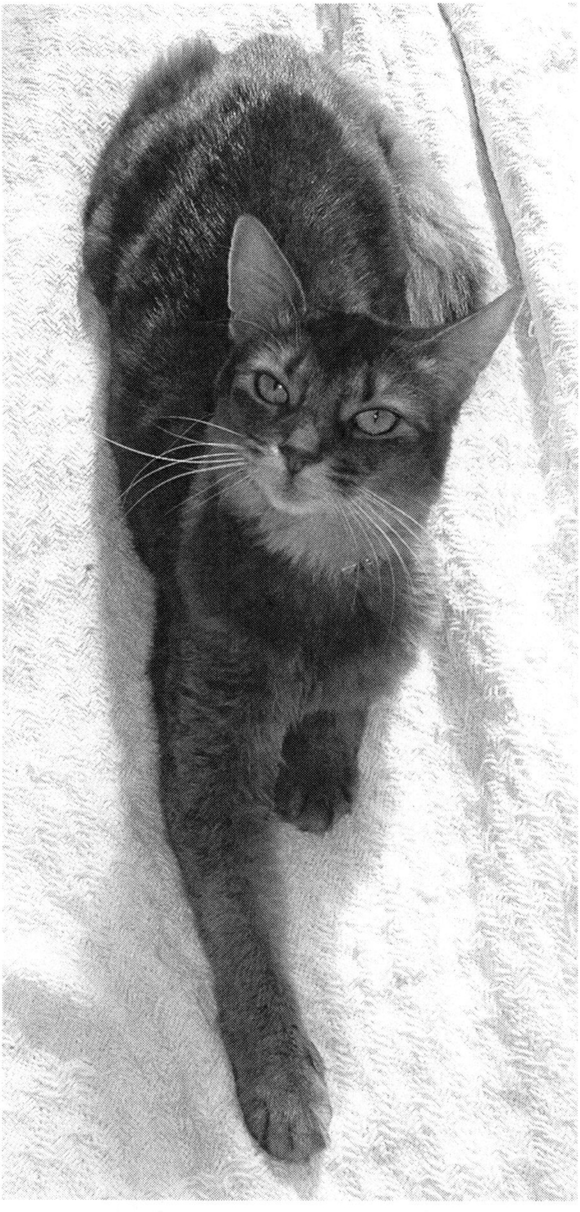

Advice From One Cat to Another

Talking Nonsense

Dear Sparkle,
I am a Siamese cat and as you know, we are great conversationalists. Unfortunately, I have a human who thinks she is talking to me, but she's not—she's just spouting off a bunch of incomprehensible gobblety-gook! I have no idea what she thinks she is doing. All I know is that when she comes home from work and I tell her what an idiot she is for being gone all day and where's my dinner, etc.—you know, just basic stuff, nothing particularly deep or interesting—she says things like, "Awww, cutie-snookums, wassa matter?" Like it's not obvious without my even having to say anything! And what's with the baby talk? I'm a cat, not a baby. In fact, I am seven so I'm not exactly a kitten either. Do you know what it's like trying to hold a conversation with someone who talks like that? Forget discussing the finer points of a good interactive cat toy or the subtle flavors of moths versus crickets. She doesn't even get it when I tell her the litter box is dirty—I might as well just make a mess on the bathroom floor if I want to get my point across. I know it's probably a lost cause, but is there any way I can make this human start talking some sense?
Signed,
Mad Meower

Dear Sparkle

Dear Mad Meower,
I completely understand your frustration. And to be honest, I doubt I have a solution that will satisfy you. You see, humans are not that bright when it comes to learning other languages. There are hundreds of different *human* languages in existence and most people only speak one. And from what I gather, even those who speak the same language often have a hard time understanding each other. So you probably can't expect your human to spend a lot of time and effort trying to learn Cat. The stupid thing is that Cat is fairly easy to speak—one just needs to learn a limited amount of vowels, be observant and use some body language. It's really much easier to learn than most human languages. Even *my* human has most of the rudimentary parts down. But I do have to admit, that little bit was a stretch for her. Cat is probably beyond the capabilities of those humans who believe baby talk is a reasonable way to carry on a discussion with their cats.

So I'm afraid that discussions about cat toys and the ever-popular moth-versus-cricket debate are out. But such topics are beyond humans anyway. They don't appreciate the exhilaration of leaping in the air after prey or the bold crunch of a bug leg in your mouth. Humans live in a colorless world, devoid of such joys. What a pity. Only another cat can understand all that. And, as you know, meows generally aren't necessary when talking with another cat. Other cats just *know* what you mean. If you want to talk to your human, as most Siamese like to do, I'm afraid you are stuck with the most banal of subjects.

Advice From One Cat to Another

On the bright side, however, you can curse at her when you are annoyed and insult her when she's done something exceptionally stupid, and she will only vaguely be aware of what you are saying. That is always amusing. And if you really can't stand the baby talk, the best thing to do is ignore her when she starts up with it. Humans hate that! Ignore her for long enough and she will drop the baby talk in favor of something a bit shriller. True, shrill human voices are annoying, but they can't keep it up for as long as they can baby talk. And it is always gratifying to get a reaction out of a human just by doing nothing!

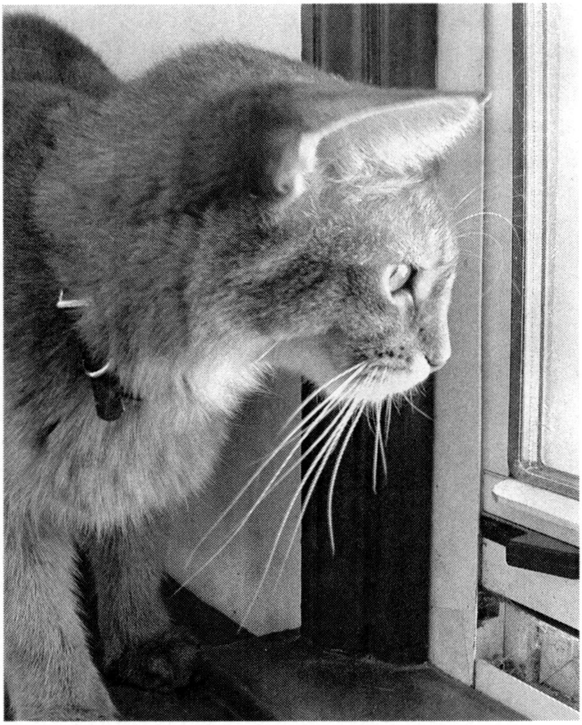

Advice From One Cat to Another

Alone and Not Loving It

Dear Sparkle,
My human has this amazing career. She runs businesses, writes books and flies all over the world to speak to large groups of people. Naturally I am the envy of every other cat in the neighborhood, but they don't know the truth of the matter. While my human's accomplishments are certainly admirable, they take her out of town quite frequently and I hate it! Every time she starts packing I freak out and get really depressed. This has been going on for the whole eight years we have been together. Last month it was even worse—we moved! I got so upset about the whole thing that I tore one of my claws. My human totally adores me—she makes that really obvious—so why does she hurt me so much by leaving all the time? If she's so important, how come she can't get all these other humans to come to her?
Signed,
Forlorn Feline

Dear Forlorn,
As much as we've tried to teach them, humans still haven't learned that their lives should completely revolve around us cats. But sometimes, of course, it would be impossible anyway. Consider this: if all the other humans came to your town to meet with your human, wouldn't they have to leave *their* cats behind? You probably didn't think of it that way!

Dear Sparkle

When you have a human with a high-powered career, the out-of-town trips are definitely a downside. The upside is that there are ways for her to make her travel less stressful on you, and since she clearly has the budget for any and all of these suggestions, she has no excuse to avoid doing them.

Humans sometimes don't realize that on top of being lonely we get really bored when left by ourselves. So yours should at least make sure you have interesting things to keep you busy while she is away. A cat tree or tower is always welcome; a couple of them are even better, especially when placed by windows of different rooms so you can check out the view. And she can make your view even better by putting bird feeders by the windows. Plus, you need to have a variety of toys especially saved for when your human goes away. Along with the usual catnip mice and crinkly balls, a really great idea is one of those hollow vinyl balls that your human can fill with treats—those are really fun to chase around! While none of this will replace your human's company, it will make your time alone a lot more entertaining.

If you were younger, like less than four years old, I would suggest that another cat would help keep you company, but at eight you are set in your ways and another cat probably would only upset you. I imagine your human already has someone looking in on you while she is away, so she needs to make sure that this person takes the time to pet and play with you and give you extra special treats.

All these activities are good for cats who suffer from an average amount of depression when their

Advice From One Cat to Another

human is on a trip. If your case of separation anxiety is more extreme, you may want to look into an anti-anxiety medication. But this is something your human should discuss with your vet—I'm just a cat, so I can't exactly dish out medical advice.

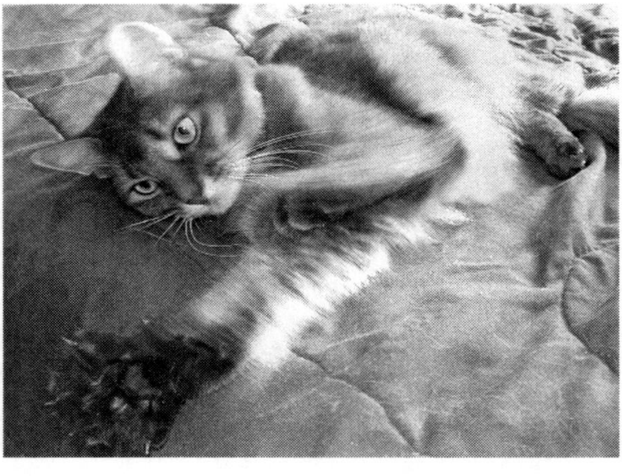

Advice From One Cat to Another

Hunting for Compliments

Dear Sparkle,
The most horrible thing just happened! But let me start at the beginning—I have this great pair of humans (at least I thought they were great) who spend a lot of time playing with me and training me how to be a great hunter. They always get these poles with cool feathery things hanging off them. I got really good at catching the feathery things and even managed to rip them off the pole a bunch of times. My humans didn't even care when I did that—they just went out and got me new toys. Since I got so good at hunting, I thought I'd show off how much I learned so I snuck out of the house one afternoon and came back with a yummy bird treat. And it wasn't some little bird, either—it was one of those big, noisy blue-feathered birds! So I came up to my humans' back door, all happy and proud with the bird in my mouth and you know what they did? They screamed at me! They told me I was a "bad cat" and a bunch of other things I don't want to repeat. What's more, they didn't even eat the bird—I think they threw it away or something. I thought they would be overjoyed that I put all this training to good use. What happened?
Signed,
Totally Freaked Out

Dear Sparkle

Dear Freaked Out,
Even if your humans didn't appreciate your catch, I do want to say that I'm impressed! If I'd been there, I would have gratefully shared your bird with you. Good job!

I'm afraid you've discovered one of the downsides of living with humans—most of them don't understand that we are natural-born hunters. When they wave those dangly, feathered toys in front of us, they think it's cute when we catch it. In reality, we're just doing what cats do—reveling in the thrill of the hunt. Ironically, they'll play with us for hours on end with these poles (at least, if we're lucky, they'll play with us for hours), and then they have a fit when we catch real, live prey. They just don't get that the live prey is even better than the toy! It's really a weird, human quirk and you are not the first cat to be mystified by it. We're all mystified by it. When it comes to hunting, the majority of humans might as well be from a different planet than us cats. In fact, I'm pretty certain they are. (I just hope they're not from the Dog Star!) Do you want to hear something totally frustrating? Way back in history we were originally prized for our ability to catch mice. Some cats that live in barns out in the country are still prized for this talent. Most modern humans, however, are like yours—I wouldn't be surprised if you lived with a pair of vegans. Ugh. How misguided. If they savored a rat or two, they'd ditch those vegetables in a second!

I know you've been traumatized by the way your humans overreacted to your awesome catch, but it was bound to happen. I'm sorry you had to be sub-

Advice From One Cat to Another

jected to such a hard lesson. So now you know that if you get the opportunity once again to hunt real, live prey to keep it to yourself. It's kind of lonely to not be able to share your prizes with your human companions, but that's one of the harsh realities of life. Just recognize that it's not because they don't love and appreciate you—they're merely clueless and misguided. Don't let it spoil your love of the hunt. Guilt never did anyone any good. Hunt with all the passion you were born with, and don't let any humans tell you any different!

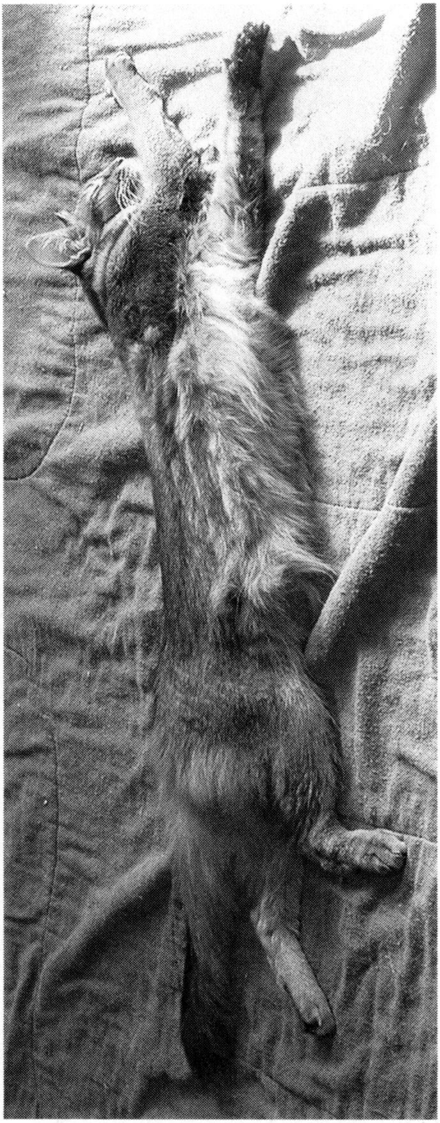

Advice From One Cat to Another

Torture Chamber Trips

Dear Sparkle,
My human tortures me when I'm sick! Last week, I wasn't feeling too great, just moping around the house. My human seemed really concerned, and I really appreciated that. But then she turned into some horrible demon—she stuffed me inside the cat carrier, paying no attention to my screams, and dragged me to that horrible place where the woman in the white coat is—my human calls her the "vet." Well, this vet put her grimy hands all over me and stuck this glass tube in a really embarrassing spot. Then she gave my human a container of this gross tasting liquid, and for the past five days she's been forcing it down my throat—like I haven't been feeling badly enough! I am feeling a little better, but now I'm wondering if my human has decided she hates me or what. I mean, why else would she treat me so badly?
Signed,
Sick and Tortured

Dear Sick,
Your human doesn't hate you. In fact she's behaving in typical human fashion—the more they care about you, the more they do things to annoy and torture you. The barbaric practice of taking us to the vet when we're ill is just one of the more extreme examples of this. I really don't understand the whole logic, or illogic, behind this, either. When

Dear Sparkle

you're sick the last thing you want is for some strange-smelling human to be poking his or her hands (and other objects) where they're not wanted. And the whole medicine thing—that's what that liquid is that your human is forcing down your throat. Yeah, it's awful stuff, but the alternative—having a pill forced down you instead—isn't much better.

The only thing I can conclude from this type of behavior is that when we're sick, humans feel so terribly helpless that they freak out and will do anything in an attempt to make us get well. It's really a testament to our patience that we tolerate it. In a perfect world, humans would figure out how to nurse us through illnesses without 1) stuffing us in a cat carrier and hauling us to the vet, 2) forcing disgusting liquids and pills on us and especially 3) coming anywhere near us with that wretched glass tube. But, I'm sad to say, this world is anything but perfect (that's what you get when humans are in charge), and so your only alternative is to let your human know of your displeasure.

Every time she finishes forcing that liquid down your throat, run off to the opposite end of the room and glare at her from afar. Don't let her even touch you for the rest of the day. If she acts hurt, then keep it up—it's working! When you see her going for the bottle of medicine, hide someplace where she will have a really difficult time extricating you. Speak to her as little as possible—only communicate to express your displeasure at being manhandled, and when you're hungry. When she finally stops giving you the medicine, give it a few more days before making up with her. She'll be so relieved she'll

Advice From One Cat to Another

probably treat you extra nicely for quite a while. Enough hints like this and maybe someday humans will figure out that they need to find new ways to treat sick cats. But probably not—they are a really dense bunch.

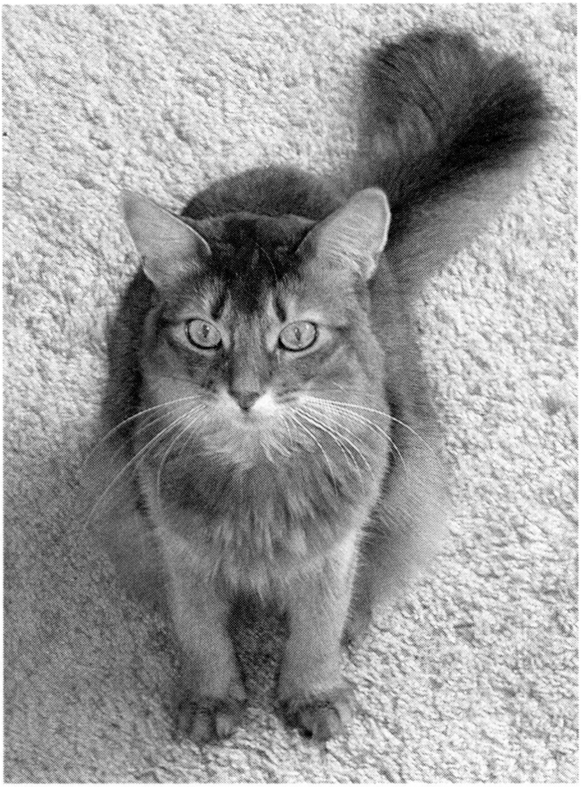

Advice From One Cat to Another

Breed Specific Myths

Dear Sparkle,
I am a Laperm—a designer cat just like you and have beautiful curls. I love my human. She's very good to me—she takes me for a walk everyday, and teaches me all sorts of tricks just like you. I have cat shelves in the house to jump on and lots of toys. But I don't think she understands my breed. She has this weird idea about a "lap cat." I have heard her talking to her friends on the phone about getting a Korat who is a "lap cat" because she wants a cat who will snuggle with her and be held. What is this confounded "lap cat" thing and how do I get it out of her head?
Signed,
Only Kitty

Dear Only,
Your human is suffering from a problem common to their species—the assumption that all cats of a specific breed will behave in expected ways. That is true only to a point. I can give you an example from my own life. My human's previous cat was completely devoted to her and her alone. So when she was looking for a new cat, she checked out breeds that were known to bond to just one person. One of those breeds happens to be the Somali, which is how she wound up with me (also she liked the way we look, and who can blame her?). Well, it's true, I do bond with one person, which happens to be my

Dear Sparkle

human. But I certainly don't worship her the way the other cat did. I mean, how can I look up to someone who exhibits such lame behavior so often? The other cat went outside and hunted and was not interested in toys, so she never realized how terrible my human is when it comes to shopping for them. And the other cat liked to be picked up. I find more often than not that getting picked up is an invasion of my space. So yeah, I "bond" with my human, if you want to call it that. Sometimes I feel more like I'm stuck with her. So she didn't get exactly what she was looking for. Personally I think she should be relieved that, for all her faults, I allow her to be my human.

Which brings me to your "lap cat" situation. Just because a certain breed is touted to be a "lap cat," that doesn't mean every last one of them will be lap cats, or at least the kind of lap cat your human desires. Korats, in fact, aren't necessarily lap cats, according to the information out there on the Internet—they're just really needy, from what I can gather, and insist on following their humans around constantly (how boring!). They also like being the main cat in the house, which is no fun for the cat that was there first. Other than that, all the information on them is conflicting—some sources say they're quiet, others say they're noisy. Some descriptions report that they're playful; others claim they're gentle and rather timid. Everyone is basing their opinion on the Korats they've encountered personally, which just shows that one breed can harbor any number of personalities within it. In fact, if you check out the Cat Fanciers Association's breed profile for Laperms, it claims you guys are lap cats!

Advice From One Cat to Another

So your human really has no idea what she wants—it's all based on conjecture. She's no more assured of getting the type of personality she wants by going after a specific breed than she would if she picked up a cat at the local pound (not that I'm trying to give her any ideas...). If she gets a second cat, it should only be as a friend to you, not something to satisfy some vague whim of hers. By the way, I don't see anything in your breed profile that says you won't play second fiddle to a Korat—perhaps you should write CFA and let them know that should be in there.

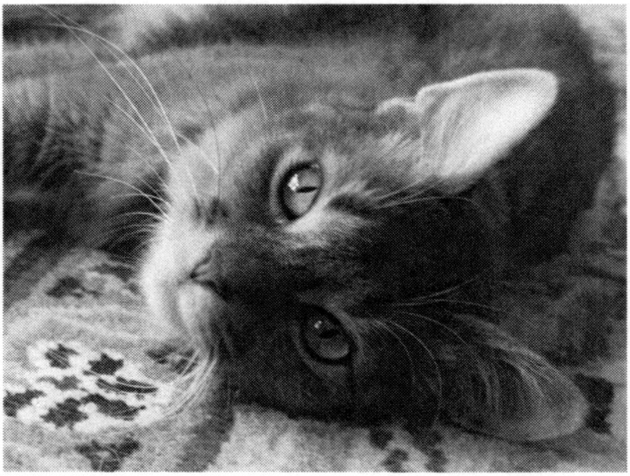

Advice From One Cat to Another

Stay Cat, Not Stray Cat

Dear Sparkle,
Apparently, I am something that humans call a "stray." At least that's what the ones I live with called me when I showed up on their doorstep asking for dinner. So I guess "stray" means "hungry, homeless kitty." The thing is that once I got the food, I decided to stick around and have all my meals there...and sleep there, and use the other's cats' toys (the other cats were not too thrilled, but never mind that). So I've pretty much moved in and it's been weeks now, but for some reason I am still being called "stray." The deal seems to be that all the humans think I should stay except for one guy called the "Dad." The dad guy keeps saying that four cats are enough and they don't need another one. (The other cats agree with him, but luckily they have no say in the matter.) He never says I have to leave, but he keeps saying that I can't stay. So how do I convince this human that I am a "stay" cat, not a "stray" cat?
Signed,
NOT a Stray!

Dear Not Stray,
Humans are really an odd bunch. They don't know when they've been licked (I suppose that's why we've been given such rough tongues—to make the licking extra obvious). You are definitely in. How do I know? Easy. The dad guy hasn't said you have to leave and it's been weeks. Trust me, you are in. That said, I

suppose you want to do something to help make it official. That is simple enough. Being a cat, you have an unlimited repertoire of cute poses and behavior. Whenever the dad guy is around, make sure you pull out all the stops. Roll around on the floor whenever he's in the room. Chirp at him and gaze at him with adoring, half-closed eyes. When he's sitting around watching television, sit next to him and purr at your loudest volume. If he reaches over to pet you, purr even louder! If you really want to lay it on thick, start following him around from room to room. For some reason, most guy humans especially like cats who behave like dogs. You will know you're successful when he starts calling you something else besides "that cat" or "that stray"—like, say, a name! When you've been given a name and everyone in the house is using it—dad guy included—there is no way you are going anywhere. The other cats will have to learn to live with you…but of course, that is a different problem for another column.

Advice From One Cat to Another

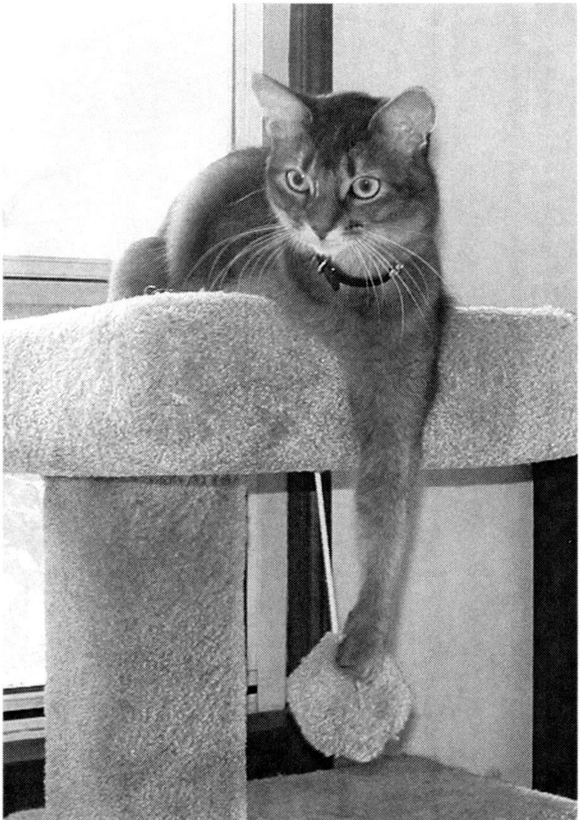

Advice From One Cat to Another

Housebound Blues

Dear Sparkle,
I used to live in this really great house that was surrounded by a big land of adventure. There were loads of trees to climb, bushes to hide in and lots and lots of butterflies to chase and birds to catch. Then something happened—I'm not sure what the whole deal was, but all of a sudden, all the furniture in the house was packed up and the humans put me in the box they use to take me to the vet. Except I didn't go to the vet. I wound up in this different house, except it has all the same furniture as before. And instead of being surrounded by a bunch of trees and bushes and stuff, there's nothing but some patches of grass and a big street. My humans won't even let me outside—they say it's "too dangerous" for me. This just won't do! I want to go back to the old house or, failing that, I'd like to at least go outside here. What can I do to get my humans to let me out? Should I use their bed as a litter box?
Signed,
Distressed

Dear Distressed,
It is no fun to move to a different home, especially when the new place isn't as nice as the old one. And it really sounds like you got the raw end of the deal here—you've basically gone from being Queen of the Jungle to living in a permanent lockdown. I don't blame you for wanting to use your humans' bed as

Dear Sparkle

a litter box. That said, leaving a "surprise" on the mattress is probably not a good idea. This kind of behavior generally does not get the desired reaction out of the humans. They may wind up confining you even further, and that would make your situation even worse. I doubt they will let you outside.

From the information you have given me, it sounds like your new home has very little yard and is located on a busy street. Your humans are probably thinking that you do not know enough to stay out of the street, and that you will be run over by a car. Since I don't know you, I can't say if you are smart enough to stay away from cars or not. Humans are poor judges of cat intelligence, so they probably don't know either (although I dare say you are probably smarter than they think you are). That said, many thousands of cats are killed by cars every year, so your humans do have cause for concern. You don't go into great detail about your old home (except for describing the delicious plethora of butterflies and birds), so I really don't know what the car situation was like there. Did you see cars much, if at all? You may be more naive about cars than you realize.

Unless you are able to escape from this new, not-so-great home and find your way back to the old one (some cats have been known to do this), I'm afraid you are just going to have to endure living in diminished circumstances. That doesn't mean you have to accept your situation as an exiled Queen gracefully. Your humans should definitely pay for what they've done to your lifestyle. So if you feel like getting your jollies by climbing the curtains,

Advice From One Cat to Another

pulling hunks of stuffing out of the couch, doing speed drills at 4 a.m. or knocking over your water dish right after it's been freshly filled, I say go right ahead. Hopefully your humans will figure out that these are the signs of a cat that needs more stimulation and will buy you loads of toys and maybe even a big cat tree or two. You had lots of fun running around outside and your humans had better make the inside of this new house pretty darn interesting. It's the least they can do for you.

Dear Sparkle

4
Culinary Delights & Disappointments

Food—a favorite topic amongst most felines. And we're just as fascinated by catching our meals as we are in its actual consumption. Sure, we enjoy the prepared food you give us (usually), but nothing beats going out and getting our own fresh food. Most humans don't even want to think about such things, and that's where they fall short. In fact, the whole food issue brings up a lot of problems in many cat households, and not just because of our love of the hunt. You'll see what I mean when you read the following letters.

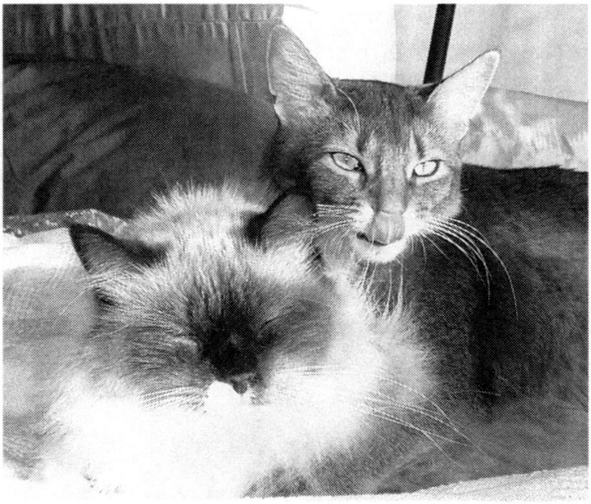

Advice From One Cat to Another

Feline Swine

Dear Sparkle,
My roommate is a pig and I don't know what to do about it! Well, he's not actually a pig—he's a cat just like me—but he hogs all the food. It happens every mealtime—my human gives us each a bowl of food, equal portions. I like to nibble, so I eat a little bit and go off and do other things. Then, when I come back, he's eaten all his and most of mine! And my human is so dense he doesn't even notice. When people point out to him that I'm so skinny and the other cat is huge, he just shrugs and says I must have a fast metabolism (whatever that is). What can I do about this situation? I'm not allowed outdoors, so I can't supplement my dinner with any birds or mice.
Signed,
Undernourished

Dear Undernourished,
You are a poor excuse for a cat! I don't mean to be harsh, but look at your situation: your roommate is hogging all the cat food and all you can do is whine about it. It's about time you puffed up, fluffed up and showed that pig who is boss! You already know that your human is completely useless. Guy humans are often like that—they tend to just dump the food down and wander off. So you have to fend for yourself. Granted, it's going to take a bit of work for a while, but part of that is your own fault for let-

Dear Sparkle

ting this situation get so out of control. Once you've really made your point, however, life should get a lot easier.

Even if you like to nibble, you can't just walk away from your food, especially with a cat like your roommate around. You'll need to keep a wary eye on your food dish, at least for now. Just eat what you normally would and leave the area, but sit somewhere where you can watch what's going on. The moment The Hog starts dipping into your food, jump him! Whap him a few times, hiss and growl. Chase him away. Take a bite of your food, just to hammer the point home (growl while you are doing this—it underscores your possessiveness), and then walk off again. But stay close. Your roommate is probably as dense as your human and won't get it the first time...or the second. You will probably have to repeat this display of dominance a few times a night for a couple of weeks before he stays away from your food for good. Really put the fear of Bast into him and show no mercy. You need to break your roommate of his bad habit once and for all. Eventually he will know better than to so much as *look* at your food dish. But even after it gets to that point, keep an eye on the situation. Your roommate may occasionally take another stab at your food dish even after you've given him a series of sound thrashings. If he tries, just attack him again—that should keep him away for a while.

Now go out there and reclaim your food dish! And stop being a whiny little wimp. Such pathetic behavior never looks good on a cat.

Advice From One Cat to Another

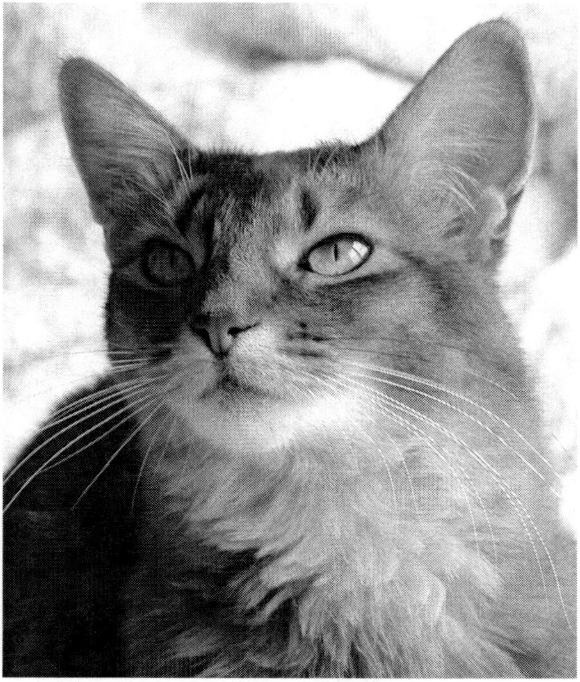

Advice From One Cat to Another

Dieting Doldrums

Dear Sparkle,
I love food—not just cat food, human food too. My humans always give me treats when they're having dinner. Steak, mashed potatoes, chicken, pasta—whatever they're having, they give me. I even get dessert. I especially like Pistachio ice cream. I get hungry just thinking about human food! But now there's a problem. The last time my humans took me to the vet (never a pleasant experience), he told them that I weighed too much. So they got special food that I have to eat. It's kind of grainy and unappealing. But what's even worse is that my humans have stopped sharing their food with me! I am hungry all the time—in fact I have to be starving to eat that disgusting diet food. How can I get my humans to give me treats again?
Signed,
More Fluff Than Fat

Dear Fluff,
I hate to tell you this, but if the vet has put you on a diet, then you are probably more fat than fluff. And as you have discovered, dieting is no fun. Look at it this way, however—being overweight can lead to all sorts of health problems, such as heart disease, diabetes, arthritis and high blood pressure. (Funny, now that I think of it, many overweight humans suffer from a lot of these problems too.) So it might be a good idea to lose a few pounds. Admittedly it's

pretty rotten that all of a sudden you just get cut off from all your favorite foods. I mean, we cats just don't have a lot of excitement in our lives. Simple pleasures like treats can go a long way to keep us happy. If your humans are smart, they will try to replace the now-absent treats with something else besides food. Interactive cat toys for example. One way to really kick your weight loss program into gear is through exercise. In fact, that's probably one of the reasons I'm so skinny—I can't get enough playtime! And I have tons of cat toys too. And a 5-foot tall cat tree. I think your humans should get you all of that, and more, to make up for the lack of food. If they keep playing with you, you will get into shape a lot quicker.

By the way, I do hope your humans are sticking strictly to the diet the vet gave them. Although you should lose weight, you need to do it slowly so you won't get an affliction called feline hepatic lipidosis (a fancy name for fatty liver disease). It can cause your liver to fail eventually. So dieting needs to be done carefully with us cats. If you really hate the diet food, maybe your humans can get you another brand; since you are the one suffering you should make them work on your behalf. At least you won't get the lousy diet food forever if you do lose the weight. Keep begging at the dinner table. Once you have dropped a pound or two maybe they will decide it's okay to give you a treat now and again. It probably won't be as much or as often as before, which means you'll just have to learn how to savor it instead of gulping it down like you probably were. But be persistent. If you bother your humans enough it will wear them out eventually, and you will get a little something for your efforts.

Advice From One Cat to Another

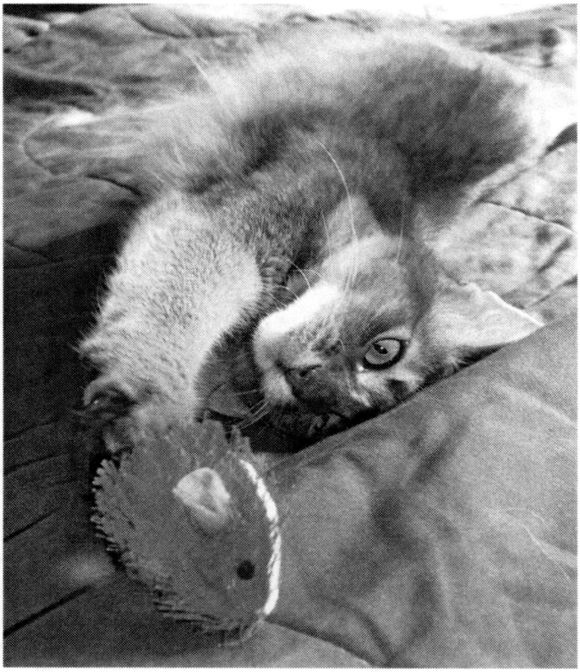

Advice From One Cat to Another

Catch of the Day

Dear Sparkle,
I really love my humans and I want to see them take better care of themselves, especially when it comes to diet. They're always pulling frozen dinners out and microwaving them. They do this almost every day! It's really unhealthy. They should be eating fresh, wholesome food instead and I've been trying to help. I go out and find them a fat, tasty mouse or a succulent bluebird, but they won't eat what I bring them. Instead they get mad. They won't even let me bring my catch into the house. What's wrong with them, and how can I get them to eat better?
Signed,
Frustrated

Dear Frustrated,
I completely understand. I mean, humans eat weird things like pizza and spaghetti and then they get grossed out when we have a fluffy moth hors d'oeuvre—there's definitely something wrong with this picture! The human diet is really something horrifying.

That said, I'm afraid you probably won't be able to get your humans to partake of your fresh catch. About the only thing they'll eat raw is sushi, which is actually nutritious and pretty yummy (except for the rice part—they really should skip the rice and just go for sashimi if you ask me). Sometimes they'll

Dear Sparkle

eat raw plants—they usually mix it up into a salad. Humans like to blend together different types of food. I know it's weird, but that's just what they do and we cats have to accept that. And to be honest, humans have different nutritional needs than we cats do. For example, a bird or a rat is a balanced meal for us—we get muscle meat, organ meat, calcium (bones), fat, and greens (whatever the creature had been eating before we pounced on it). Humans actually need more carbohydrate than this. Smart humans will eat lots of plants and some grains for their carbs. The not-so smart humans skip the greens and load up on bread and cake and pastries—that's too many carbs, even for them. Actually, some people have adopted the cat way of eating—lots of meat and not many carbs—and they call it the "Atkins diet." But unfortunately, even those people won't eat the mice and birds you bring home.

Since your humans get so upset when you bring your catch home, you probably shouldn't even bother. They don't appreciate it, so just eat it yourself. It's not that they're ingrates—they honestly don't understand. As for making them eat better—well, humans are pretty stubborn, but there are a few tricks you can try. Whenever you see that your humans are about to eat something really bad, like a piece of pie or a cheese Danish, leap up on the table and bat it onto the floor. Keep in mind that the first few times you do this, they will probably get mad and yell at you. But if you are consistent in what you knock over, they may eventually get the idea that you know what food is bad for them. If you never do it with the chicken breast, but you always do it with the chocolate cake, they're bound to put two and two

Advice From One Cat to Another

together. If they won't listen to you and, in fact, start locking you away whenever they sit down to eat, I guess you'll just have to accept their curious eating habits. But don't let that stop you from giving them a dirty look whenever they have cookie breath.

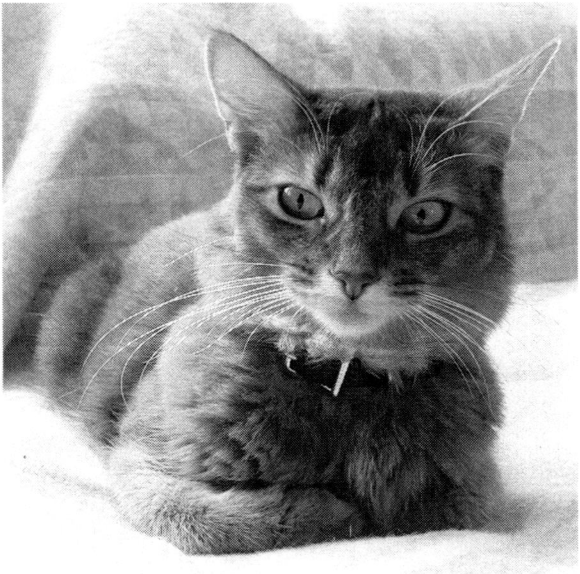

Advice From One Cat to Another

Getting Yours on Thanksgiving

Dear Sparkle,
I have a real dilemma here. Every year around this time my family cooks up a storm. Among other things, they roast a huge bird carcass. I mean *huge*! They call it a turkey or something. Anyhow, every year I see this beautiful, glistening bird...and I never get any! Nor do I get any of the other good stuff my humans cook up. They just dump the usual cheap kibble in my bowl like any other day. How do I get a piece of the action?
Signed,
Famished

Dear Famished,
Wait a minute—did I hear you say that your humans only feed you *kibble*? You mean, the cheap, dry stuff from the supermarket? And then they don't give you any turkey? That's practically cruelty! Really, you should report them to the ASPCA. I feel bad for you.

Yes, you certainly deserve some turkey during human holiday time, but you also need to keep a few things in mind. Humans eat a lot of food that's actually toxic to cats—onions for example. If they stick onions in the pan while roasting the turkey (not something I'd personally recommend, by the way), then you should avoid it. Or if they load it up with garlic. We cats don't take too well to large amounts of garlic, either. Other foods you should avoid include coffee, chocolate, alcohol, yeast dough, grapes, raisins, mushrooms, peppers and large amounts of salt. Check things out in the kitchen while the cooking is going on, and don't even think of begging for any dishes that include these items.

Now back to the turkey. If it's non-toxic, you certainly should get some. In my household we get some of the giblets—they come in a bag inside the turkey. It's sort of the equivalent to the organ meat of the normal size birds you may catch on your neighborhood rounds, if you're an outdoor cat. It's good stuff. We don't get all of it, however—my human saves the best parts and cuts them up to put in the stuffing (this really burns me, by this way). Obviously, your humans aren't considerate enough to even toss you a few giblet chunks, so you may have to take matters into your own paws. Success in an endeavor like this comes down to timing, so pay attention to my instructions.

Don't go after the turkey when it first comes out of the oven. I know it smells incredible and looks inviting, but there are a lot of good reasons to wait. First of all, it's really hot and you could burn yourself. Plus, it's not carved yet, so it'll be more difficult to grab any meat—you can't tear off pieces with the speed you'll need. And, as you're no doubt aware, you'll get in trouble. You'll get in trouble regardless, of course, but you'll get in the worst trouble if you try to tackle the turkey before the humans have had a chance to have any of it. Wait until they've carved the turkey and served it. Then give your humans one last chance to redeem themselves by wandering

Advice From One Cat to Another

around the table and begging. If you know how to sit up, you might try that—humans think this is really special. If none of this works, and you are still turkeyless, then wait until everyone has finished eating. There will usually be quite a bit of turkey left over. Once the humans have left the table, keep one eye on the turkey. The trick is, you'll be the only one paying attention to the turkey—the humans are stuffed and probably don't even want to look at it anymore. As soon as you notice that their attention has drifted away, or better yet, if they've left the vicinity of the turkey altogether, go! Leap up, grab the biggest hunk of turkey you can sink your teeth into and make a run for it! Now hide somewhere where no one can get you, and if anyone even tries, growl at them. That should put them off. Once you are done, you can come out again. Prove that you can let bygones be bygones by flopping on the ground and rolling playfully on your back. If you're lucky, they'll think it's cute and forgive you right away.

One last note—avoid the bones when you make your mad dash. Cooked turkey bones aren't pliable like the bones of freshly killed birds. Cooked bones are loaded with splinters and they're dangerous. Eat 'em and you may wind up at the emergency clinic. It's best to go for hunks of meat that have been sliced or have fallen off the bone. Good luck and happy turkey hunting!

Dear Sparkle

5
Kitty Quirks

Humans think we cats have it easy—we sleep much of the day, play when we want and have our meals served to us by our own personal maids and butlers. But appearances are deceiving. A cat's life can be very stressful. True, much of our stress is due to our humans—they change partners and homes without consulting us, bring home other creatures without our consent and change our brand of food and litter just because they happen to have one of those coupon things. We cats are supposed to be independent beings, and all of this is a reminder that our humans can screw things up for us royally at a moment's notice. So is it any wonder that on occasion, we are driven just the slightest bit crazy? When that happens, I get pleas for help like the ones you are about to read.

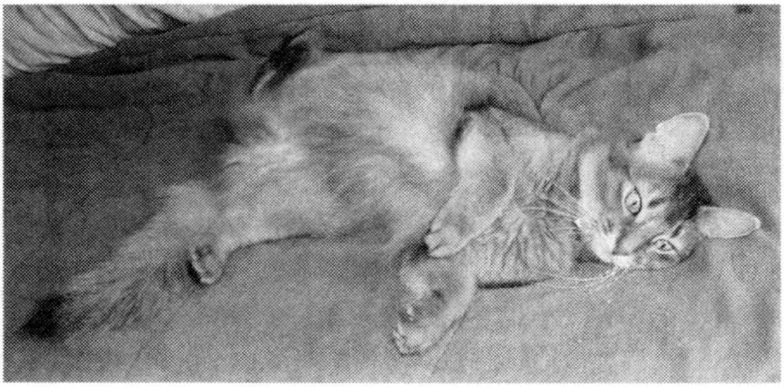

Advice From One Cat to Another

The Brush Off

Dear Sparkle,
I have long, beautiful fur and I groom it constantly. For some reason, my human doesn't think I'm doing a good enough job, so she keeps grabbing me and brushing me. Granted, I do occasionally miss a few places and sometimes I get knots, but it hurts when she starts yanking on them. In fact, I hate the whole brushing process. It really gets on my nerves. Should I just whap her a few times whenever she comes near me with that brush? Or is there another way to get her to put that thing away and leave me alone?
Signed,
Unbrushable Me

Dear Unbrushable,
Although you really hate being brushed, there are quite a few cats out there who do like it. Personally I can take it or leave it depending on my mood, but more often than not it feels good to me. I think that maybe your human doesn't really know how to brush you, and that is what's causing you so much grief. Is she using one of those "slicker" brushes? That's generally not the right kind of brush for a longhaired cat like you. Shorthaired cats usually love the slicker because they can feel the little metal tines skritching and massaging their skin. But slickers will just glide over long fur and frankly are not very effective. It feels like the human is doing

Dear Sparkle

nothing, and really, she is. But before you start taking random swipes at your human every time she shows up with that dreaded brush, see if you can get her to take a look over here to find out what the right type of brushing tools are for you. Seriously, if you're getting knots and dreads, you really *aren't* doing a very good job and could use some help. Your human can be of use in this area if she receives the proper training.

First, she needs to drop the current brush she's using and get a bristle brush cats. Plus she'll need some metal combs—one with wide teeth, one with medium teeth, and one with fine teeth (the latter one is for fleas if, God forbid, you ever get them). Combs pick up more loose fur and go through long hair better. If you're really fluffy, like my roommate Boodie, you'll do well with a shedding blade or a rake type comb too—it'll get at the loose undercoat fur, and there's probably a lot more of that than you could possibly imagine. I mean, if you were to actually groom all that off yourself, you'd be coughing up serious hairballs. So let your human do it (groom your fur, not cough up hairballs). As for the knots, she needs to be careful—if she pulls on them, then she does deserve to be whapped. Matted fur needs to be worked over carefully with a comb and cut away cautiously with blunt-edged scissors. It's not something that any lamebrain human can do—maybe someone who has better grooming skills can show yours how to do it. If you're treated with the care and skill you deserve, there's no reason for you to hate being groomed. You may even learn to like it!

Advice From One Cat to Another

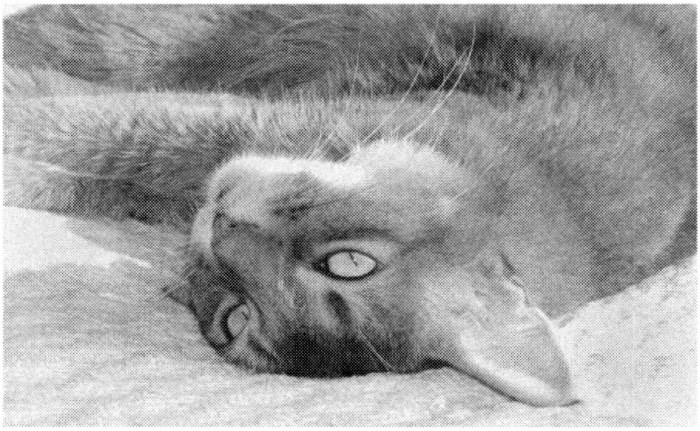

Advice From One Cat to Another

OCD Kitty

Dear Sparkle,
My human is concerned about me because I keep pulling my hair out. I don't see what the big deal is, really—I am fastidious and like to be clean! My human certainly doesn't know much about keeping me clean—you should have seen what happened the one time she tried to wash me! But that was a long time ago, when I was a kitten, and I'm 10 years old now. I have been careful to groom myself meticulously ever since, but I've been doing it more frequently since my best pal—a dog, actually!—moved away. He went with my human's former boyfriend and now I don't see either of them anymore. Since I am quite doglike myself—I often take walks with my human—I think we are okay without the dog (and the boyfriend), but I still feel an emptiness in my heart. My human thinks this might be why I keep pulling my hair out. What do you think?
Signed,
Grief-Stricken Groomer

Dear Grief-Stricken,
You have had a load of stress in your life, and I think you are in a bit of denial about it. Anyone who lost a friend is going to be upset, and every cat has his or her own way of expressing it. More often than not, we'll be depressed for a period of time, but we will move on. There are times, however, when the loss is so upsetting that it winds up causing some bizarre

Dear Sparkle

behavior. The big problem is when that the behavior becomes ingrained. My human calls it an "obsessive-compulsive disorder." Apparently this happens to humans too. But who cares about them—I'm here to discuss cat problems, not the puny foibles of humans.

Your hair-pulling compulsion is not uncommon. The noted veterinarian Dr. Nicholas Dodman (he wrote the book *The Cat Who Cried for Help*) says it's called "psychogenic alopecia." Some cats pull out nearly all their fur and swallow so much of it that they are always hacking up hairballs. Some even make themselves bleed. This isn't any way for a cat to live! You are probably not even fully aware of how miserable you are. Unfortunately, there is not much your human can do by herself to help you. She can try to distract you with love and play when you feel the need to groom too much, but this is usually not enough to bring your behavior to an end. What you really need (and I know you're going to hate me for this) is professional help. That's right—a trip (or several) to the veterinarian.

The vet will rule out any physical problems that may be causing your excessive grooming and hair pulling. (It's always a possibility that you could be suffering from fleabites, or have an as-yet undiagnosed skin problem.) If in fact your problem is obsessive-compulsive, the vet will probably recommend an anti-anxiety medication. There are several options, so if one doesn't work, maybe another drug will. You will probably only have to take these drugs temporarily, so hopefully your human won't be shoving medicine down your throat forever. Per-

Advice From One Cat to Another

sonally, I think that would be far more stressful than what you are already going through! But if it's only for a while, you'll just have to buckle down and deal, and realize that brighter days are ahead.

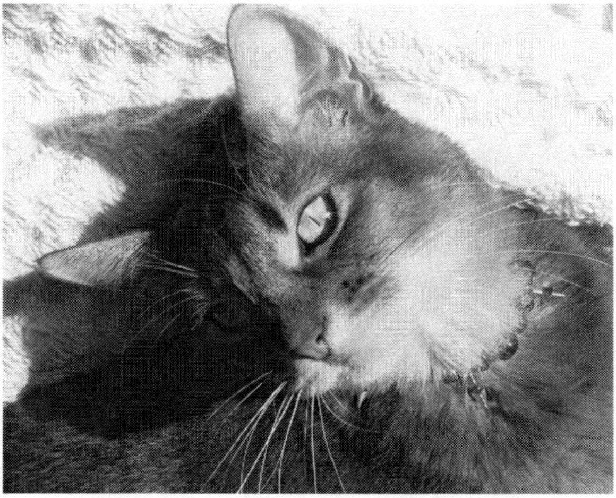

Advice From One Cat to Another

Beauty and the Battle Scars

Dear Sparkle,
I hate to brag, but I am truly a gorgeous cat. I have long, pretty fur, a big ruff and a very fluffy tail. Because of this, humans often think I'm lazy and pampered but nothing could be farther from the truth. In fact, I spend most of my days scanning my neighborhood for any strange cats, and if I see any I beat them up! No cat is allowed within a 100-yard radius of my home unless I say so (and I rarely say so). The only problem is that sometimes all this fighting gets in the way of my looking my best. A few weeks ago I came home bleeding and just the other day I broke a tooth and the vet had to take it out. I need to figure out how to hide these flaws so that they don't mar my good looks. Any suggestions?
Signed,
Tough but Beautiful

Dear Tough,
Hmm. You do talk a good game, but it sounds like every now and again, someone's getting the best of you. As loathe as you may be to admit it, no cat wins a hundred percent of the battles she engages in. So you might as well get real: you can't be a winner all the time and you can't go out fighting all the other cats in the neighborhood and expect to look glamorous. It's one or the other—beauty or brawn. Either take your licks and nicks or stay home and spend your days grooming.

Dear Sparkle

What should be a bigger concern is having your human check you out periodically for any hidden, infected bites that might turn into abscesses. Since you are a fluffy cat, one of your foes could nail you good and no one would be any the wiser until the infection started getting really bad. Usually, though, if there is a sore under your fur, it will hurt when touched—if your humans pet you and you react by yelling out and biting them, that should give them a clue that something's wrong underneath the fluff. Granted, if you do get an abscess, the vet will probably have to shave the wounded area and you may even have to wear a cone while it heals. This will definitely mar your beauty, at least for a while. But like I said, that comes with the territory when you want to be a tough cat. Beauty is important, but your health is essential.

Speaking of health, is your territory really all that important to you? Indoor cats (like me), on the average, have a lifespan of 14 years while outdoor cats often only live to be four (or less). Outdoor cats like yourself risk contracting serious illnesses from stray cats, being eaten by coyotes, getting attacked by strange dogs, suffering torture from evil, cruel humans, or getting hit by a car. None of this happens to us indoor cats. Granted, not every cat is happy staying indoors, but most of us adjust and are perfectly fine with it. It's just something to think about.

Advice From One Cat to Another

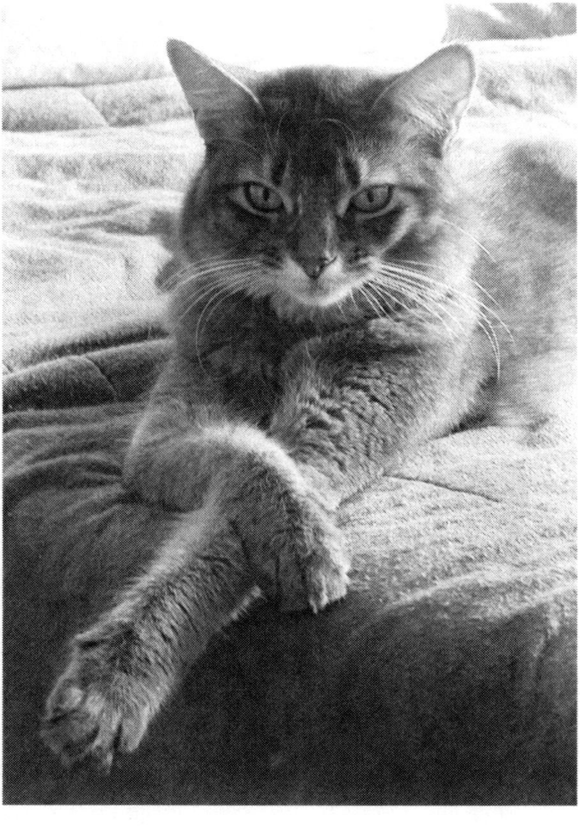

Advice From One Cat to Another

Comforting Compulsions

Dear Sparkle,
I was separated from my birth mommy too early. I think that she was sick. When my human found me I was only five weeks old and I had been abandoned. So now every time I get into a "comfortable" situation (anything that makes me purr) I start drooling. Then I start licking and trying to nurse on whatever I'm licking. It started off just being the comforter that my human sleeps under (since I love to sleep in her bed!) but now I'll lick whatever it is that's around when I start purring. I know that these impulses are caused by the natural instincts to feel nurtured when I'm feeling good, but what can I do to stop licking every blanket in sight?
Signed,
Mommy's Cat

Dear Mommy's Cat,
Humans are strange when it comes to how they feel about cats who lick and suck. Sometimes they think the habit is kittenish and cute, but eventually they start getting annoyed, which I really don't understand—I mean, why do they coo over something one moment and then get mad at us later on for doing the very same thing? Occasionally it has to do with—as they put it—"ruining" a blanket or sweater...as if they have a better use for it than we do. You don't say whether your human is starting to give you a hard time about your licking habit but

Dear Sparkle

since you wrote to me I figure that maybe she has. And of course that means the two of you need to come to an agreement. Compromise is one of the downsides of cohabitating with humans.

Hopefully your human realizes that nothing is going to stop your licking and sucking habit completely, but she can do things to keep herself happy without cramping your style too much. One thing she can do—and this is actually pretty cool—is distract you with toys when you start getting too fixated on a blanket. Most of the time playing is actually a lot more fun than licking a blanket. Or she can designate one small blanket as being yours and yours alone and gently nudge it under your mouth every time you start your licking habit. That way you're only "destroying" one blanket, and you still get to have your little blissful moments. In a pinch, if she really doesn't want you sucking something in particular, she can blow in your face.

I've heard some people recommend really nasty things, like making loud noises every time a cat displays this behavior, or spraying the cat with water, or putting bad-tasting stuff on the fabric that the cat is licking. In my opinion, these are not acceptable solutions. They are mean and show no respect for us cats. Maybe putting something bitter on an electrical cord is okay—after all, that's for our own safety—but not when we're in such a pleasantly comfortable and dreamy state. But of course, that's just my own opinion.

One thing that may be a concern is your drooling. Sometimes cats who lick and suck will drool

Advice From One Cat to Another

because their actions feels so good, but it could also indicate that you need to have your mouth looked at. You could be developing gingivitis or tooth decay, and if that's the case it should be addressed. Even relatively young cats can have mouth problems, and gum diseases can lead to other serious illnesses in cats (humans too).

Lastly, be careful about getting really obsessive about your licking and sucking. While humans seem to take a lot of enjoyment in complaining about things we cats do, there are times when a habit really does get out of hand. If that is the case with you, then you may need to consult with your vet about medication. Cats will occasionally develop obsessive-compulsive disorder (I think it's because humans drive us up a wall), and drugs actually can help.

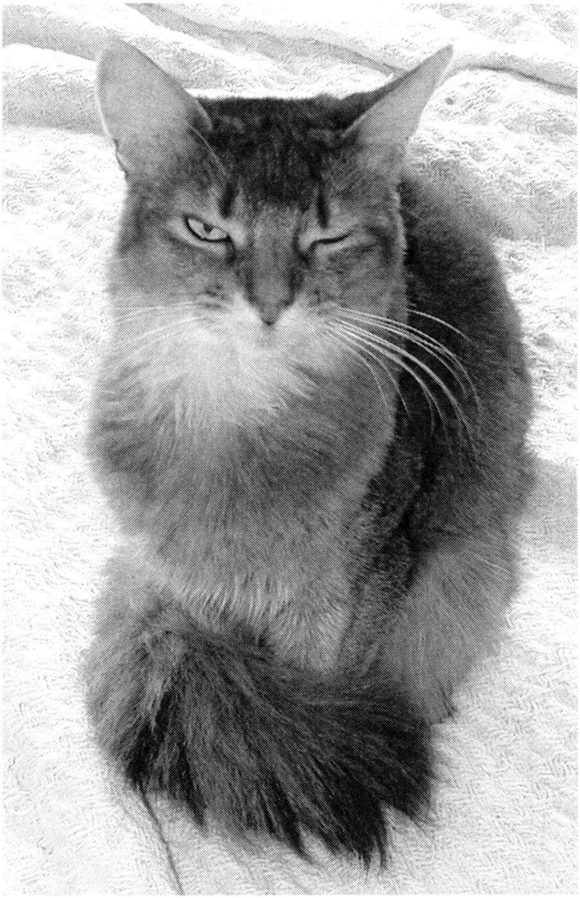

ABOUT THE AUTHOR

Sparkle the Designer Cat is a ruddy Somali of grand champion lineage: her father, GC Tajhara's Miles Davis, was a show winner and cover cat for the May 2001 issue of *Cat Fancy* magazine. Sparkle was one of 4 siblings born on June 24, 2002. In October of that year, at the age of four months, Sparkle moved from her hometown of Temecula, California to glitzy, glittery Los Angeles. Her good looks were noticed almost from the start and before long she became a supermodel. Not satisfied to skate by merely on her lean, elegant appearance, she has also earned fame as a prominent online diarist and advice columnist. Her website, Sparkle the Designer Cat (http://www.sparklecat.com) is read by cat and human fans from all over the world. Sparkle resides in a fashionable district of Los Angeles with two humans, two feline roommates and, unfortunately, a dog. *Dear Sparkle* is her first book.

Want more of Sparkle's wit and wisdom?
Join Sparkle's Designer Cat Fan Club
It's FREE!

When you become a member of Sparkle's Designer Cat Fan Club, you're not only on the inside track of all things Sparkle, you also get:

- A monthly email newsletter containing Sparkle's tips, links and more!
- A special members-only link to a downloadable, full-color, full-page calendar—new each month!
- Coupons and special promotions from many popular pet-related online merchants!
- Fan club-only contests—win copies of Sparkle's books, calendars, cat toys and other exciting prizes!
- A special Fan Club banner you can add to your blog or website!
- And even more cool stuff, not to mention bragging rights.

If this is all catnip to your senses, then sign up! Joining Sparkle's Designer Cat Fan Club is easy—just visit her website at **www.sparklecat.com** and find the "Fan Club" link. Enter your email address and you'll become part of an exclusive group of feline fanatics who are always a step ahead of the rest. There are no special qualifications to be a member—a true Designer Cat is made, not born! Ferals, purebreds and especially shelter cats—we are all Designer Cats at heart!

Visit www.sparklecat.com
Become a Designer Cat today!

Printed in the United Kingdom by
Lightning Source UK Ltd., Milton Keynes
141237UK00001B/37/P